Whatever Happened to

CHRISTIAN EVANGELISM?

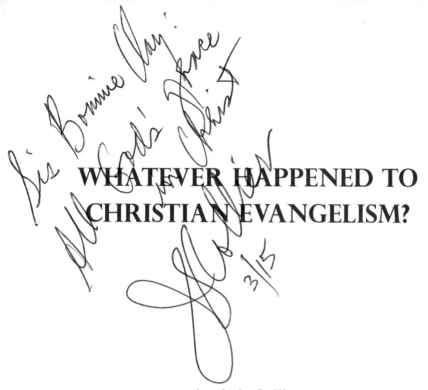

WHATEVER HAPPENED TO CHRISTIAN EVANGELISM?

Jarvis L. Collier

Townsend Press

Sunday School Publishing Board
Nashville, Tennessee

Published by Townsend Press
Nashville, Tennessee
© 2014 by Jarvis L. Collier

ISBN 978-1-939225-23-8

TABLE OF CONTENTS

Mrs. Ellen R. Jones—my mother,
who modeled sharing
our faith in Christ before me.
Bless you forever!

ACKNOWLEDGEMENTS

My life has always been in the hands of God. Before my earliest awareness, He was molding and shaping me as a vessel for His glory. Continually, I am amazed at the wonder of His grace, a plan that included me in the beloved in Christ. Further, before the gift of writing was even fully formed, I felt God's promptings to share revelation, insight, and application with a wide audience. Praise the Lord, for "birthing" another book, for His glory!

My church, the Pleasant Green Baptist Church, in Kansas City, Kansas, has heard it all before: "There are many churches bigger, but none better than you." That sentiment means that we value excellence, character, godliness, prayer, professionalism, courtesy, punctuality, respect, and dignity, all in Christ. Most of all, we value people, broken yet valuable in the sight of God. Thank you to the best "team" in the world. You make me a better Christian leader.

Special recognition goes to my church staff: Ethel Davis, for untiring devotion to our total ministry in Christ; Bernice McKinney, for assisting me in all pastoral tasks for the kingdom of God; Lucy Harmon, for handling many critical functions; the Office of the Pastor team, for research, transcribing, editing and more. You are simply the best!

I bless the Lord for Helen Gray, whose keen eyes, helpful suggestions, discerning eyes, and prayerful ways immeasurably assisted this project.

Equally true, our church family represents the everyday "laboratory" for these evangelism concepts. Over a few years, God has blessed us with new faces, new ministries, new outreaches, and new dynamism, all by following Him and "fishing" for souls. And, know this: what's coming is better than what's been!

I sincerely appreciate a cadre of Christian colleagues who patiently listened as I laid out the central thrust of this book. Recommended books, articles, lectures, late phone calls, mini-debates and inquiries have led to the finished product. Along the way, you sharpened my perspective.

Finally, to my wife, Jennifer, and my children, Jarvis II and Jillian, thank you for allowing me to stay late at the office, as I tried to capture what God put on my heart for evangelism. You sacrifice so much in helping me fulfill my calling in Christ. "Family night" is precious time!

INTRODUCTION

In advancement of the central thesis of this book—that saints of God must share their Christian faith with the lost—some dear friends have wondered as to the source of my passion. Perhaps Shakespeare's words encapsulate it: *"There is a tide in the affairs of men which, taken at the flood leads to fortune. Omitted, all the voyage of their life is bound in shallows and in miseries."* With all my heart, I assert, the Christian faith stands at its "flood" moment. Accordingly, we must evangelize the lost, or else Christianity might "fossilize" as a once-great movement.

Clearly, the Christian faith will never be extinct from the earth, as so many adherents will continually trust God, affirming new life in Christ. However, like so many churches in European cities, the Christian witness may become greatly diminished, to the point that our buildings will lie empty, bereft of worshipful vitality, stark reminders of a once-vibrant era. Indeed, if something ails American Christianity, the truth is its remedy can be found in a return to energetic evangelism, seen in new converts to the way of the kingdom of God, established through submission to Christ alone.

So, this book represents a clarion call to the total Christian witness—leaders, congregations, denominations, academies—to return to our seminal calling from God: *"Be My witnesses,"* *(Acts 1:8), along with its concomitant, "make disciples"* (Matthew 28:19). Reaffirming these twin emphases with tangible actions by all components of the church of the Lord Jesus Christ will infinitely enhance the kingdom of God. The Christian evangelism effort should be well on its way; but, now represents a great time to get started!

At the same time, this book represents an attempt to prompt more of those in league with the Master, to disseminate His grace, love, forgiveness, acceptance and peace to the masses of humanity. In short, I hope my efforts here will prompt every reader to get the word out: Christ saves all who commit their lives to Him. No matter the background, circumstances, past failures, mistakes, or sins—every person can start anew with the Savior. That simple yet profound message colors everything I believe and everything for which I stand.

From early in my Christian life (as a young boy) until the present, as I matured in life and in Christian understanding, the constant has been a sense of the singular importance of Christian evangelism: *"proclamation of the good news of salvation in Jesus Christ with a view to bringing about the reconciliation of the sinner to God the Father through the regeneration of the Holy Spirit."* It has also been my fervent conviction that this proclamation must be done by every saint of God, all within the body of Christ.

This book represents, then, my attempt to prompt more saints toward personal evangelistic engagement. It is my central thesis that the Word of God gives all the essential elements for Christian evangelism: mandate, means, manpower, mission, motivation, message and manifestation. Within these "M's," we should find ways to present God's grace in Christ.

If this book resonates, then, more saints in the pews will be inspired by the example of our Savior, Jesus Christ. Additionally, multiple Scriptures affirm evangelism as the dominant motif for Christian outreach. In short, after personal salvation there should be an overwhelming desire to bring the lost, and the unsaved into the consuming "joy of the Lord."

A brief history of Christian evangelism over the last half century will be presented here. We will aim to answer the question as to why Christian evangelism has lost its "edge," among many competing interests. Further, we will offer ways to engage the pew in deliberate outreach to the unsaved. Moreover, we will, it is hoped, finally destroy the myth that people today are, in fact, not lost without Christ as Savior. Indeed, they are! Employment, housing, health, security, freedom, and friendship are not enough to build "life" upon.

In our journey chronicled here, we shall emphasize the centrality of Jesus Christ as Savior, found in the greater New Testament portrait of Him. Indeed, I fully rest upon the biblical foundation: *"And there is salvation in no one else; for there is no other name under heaven that has been given among men, by which we must be saved"* (Acts 4:12, NASB). This embodies, then, a Jesus-centered book; and I am, unapologetically, a Jesus-preacher!

Along the way, we will analyze and evaluate various approaches of Christian evangelism (personal, intellectual, testimonial, relational, media, mass and invitational). Beyond debate, we must find the style which accords with the willing evangelist, and then employ it. My objective here involves deployment of God's people, like a conquering army, to "win some" to Christ.

As the contemporary Christian faith community embraces evangelism to a heightened degree, it will promote obedience to God, dynamism, numerical increase, greater focus, and the expansion of the kingdom of God through our Savior, Jesus Christ.

Finally, saints of God are left with inescapable truth from Christ: *"The harvest (souls for salvation) is plentiful, but the workers are few. Therefore beseech the Lord of the harvest to send out workers into His harvest"* (Matthew 9:37-38, NASB). Avoiding evasion, rhetoric, insularity, apathy, and laziness, Christian leaders, congregants, congregations, academies, and denominations must determine their obedience to God in the area of evangelism.

Amid current confusion, Christians must offer strong biblical, spiritual, intellectual, practical responses to lost persons among us. My prayer is that this book will assist in that worthy objective. As you read, I welcome your reactions (from intense disagreement to fulsome approval). However, what I pray against is continued reluctance by the body of Christ, as millions languish in their lost condition. Supported by the Word of God, I sincerely believe the lost and the unsaved are headed to eternal separation from God, if they do not embrace Christ as their personal Savior. And more saints of God must declare that sobering message, along with the good news regarding Christ: He saves!

CHAPTER 1

Whatever Happened to Christian Evangelism?

At present, in my middle-aged years, having followed Christ since the time of a young child (now, spanning over forty-five years), I am enjoying Christian ministry as never before. God is achieving great works for His kingdom, using flawed creatures such as us. Indeed, the Scripture holds true: *"We have this treasure in earthen vessels, that the surpassing greatness of the power may be of God and not from ourselves"* (2 Corinthians 4:7).

Of late, however, I have arrived at an unsettling, sobering conclusion: the Christian family across America seems to have lost its understanding of, passion for, and urgent pursuit of Christian evangelism. Simply put, enthusiasm for sharing Jesus Christ in the power of the Holy Spirit with the lost, the un-churched, those formerly in the Christian fold, and others seems to have dissipated. Currently, millions of sincere saints of God live a personalized, insular, and minimal form of Christianity: chiefly preoccupied with their private devotion to God (sanctification, marriage, healing,

5

breakthrough, material prosperity). Unfortunately, there is insufficient concern by dedicated saints for those alienated from God, mired in sin, broken, guilt-ridden, and confused, sorely in need of the Savior.

From the late 1960s through the '90s, the Christian worldview was greatly influenced by national luminaries: Billy Graham (evangelistic crusades), Bill Bright (Campus Crusade for Christ), D. James Kennedy (Evangelism Explosion), E.V. Hill (revivals/conferences), Jerry Falwell (pastor and chancellor, Liberty University) John MacArthur (pastor and president, Master's College), Tony Evans (pastor, author), and prominent Southern Baptist clergy. While they represented diverse branches of Christianity, they shared a passion for teaching, training, and deploying the Christian family to reach the lost and the unsaved with saving truth, pivoting on a simple yet sublime message: Christ as the only way to a relationship with the eternal God.

As several of these aforementioned leading voices on evangelism have retired, with some growing older, while some have made their transition to the bosom of the Lord, there is a great vacuum of national leadership on Christian evangelism. Unfortunately, few national Christian voices seem to be interested in articulating a clear, compelling, coherent message on the importance of leading millions of Christians on a national crusade designed to reach the unsaved in our country, and globally. This book and other evangelistic tools are necessary means of challenging and calling out Christian leaders on this critical subject. Where and when Christian leaders command respect, attention, influence, and sway over other Christian leaders and congregations, they must use such to call the body of Christ to its first, highest, and ultimate priority: leading millions of unsaved to the wonders of salvation through the Lord Jesus Christ.

Due to the power of God working in these "Gospel giants" and others, for thirty years, Christian evangelism served as the overriding compulsion of the Christian movement. The national environment was saturated by tangible concern for reaching the lost, drawing in the unsaved. Over and again, Christian leaders, theologians, writers, and congregations spoke of *"soul-winning," "witnessing," "sharing our faith," "canvassing for souls"* and the like. Evangelism tracts were plentiful; evangelism-training conferences were held; evangelistic revivals called sinners to repentance. The evangelistic concern was synonymous with the calling of Christians to service everywhere. In that wonderful period, the mandate, mission, message, and motivation of the Christian church seemed clear, concise and compelling.

During these decades, as a teenager and then a young adult, I vividly recall being guided by an evangelistic thrust which found me on many occasions talking to complete strangers regarding their Christian commitment or the lack thereof. During those years, I and others in our congregation were engaged in a regular practice of going door-to-door (like the Jehovah's Witnesses), only with a clear message of traditional, biblical witness to the unique Son of God, Jesus Christ. As many regard their diet and bodily exercise, we sensed a "healthy" Christian would go after the unsaved. Jesus' persuasive paradigm, *"Follow Me, and I will make you fishers of men"* (Matthew 4:19) resonated in our spirits, driving us to "hit the streets," seeking lost humanity!

To undergird my faith and furnish me with tools for evangelistic success, I remember reading and re-reading the

[Handwritten annotation: MEET ME AT MY POINT OF NEED BEFORE ELEVATING ME TO YOU.]

Word of God. I remember stirring calls by passionate Christian ministers to evangelize the lost. I remember powerful altar calls, where in a single worship, 300 youth might commit their lives to Christ. I remember the sense that I was working for the Master, exemplifying Him and advancing the kingdom of God. Not surprisingly, then, those years were thrilling, captivating, joyous, and full. Convinced of the mandate to evangelize from Scripture, I welcomed any opportunity to usher others into eternity, fully prepared to meet their God. While those days were quite heady, I enjoyed using evangelistic tools such as the *"Four Spiritual Laws"* booklet and the *"??"* lapel pin. At the same time, Christian films (*A Thief in the Night* among them) depicted Christ's rapture of saints, and the necessity for all humanity to be prepared for the second coming of the Savior.

An entire Christian generation, then, gauged their effectiveness on conversions, baptisms, numbers won to Christ, multiple worships, mass crusades, revivals, times of spiritual refreshing/renewal, Christian retreats and evangelism conferences. Let me quickly answer those who assert that Christianity is greater than numbers (often those without quantifiable increase in worship attendance). Indeed, Christian success involves alignment of one's life with the person and teachings of the Lord Jesus Christ in a life of worship, prayer, service, surrender and obedience to the will of God, and the extension of the kingdom of God. Nevertheless, the Bible affirms numbers, as Acts records the geographic expansion of the Christian movement (3,000 saved in Acts 2:41). *[Handwritten annotation: Done by Holy Spirit]*

If God still moves by the proclamation of Christ (and He does!) as Savior, then, perhaps any Christian congregation might expect at least three converts per Lord's Day.

Equally important during those years, there seemed Christian unanimity in that people were, indeed, lost in their sin, not because of personal error alone but, more critically, because they had failed to repent, accept the plan of God, by not embracing Christ as Savior. Since then, the entire notion of the lost condition of humanity has been seriously undermined. Now, in the name of religious tolerance, just about any "spiritual" or "religious" expression is celebrated, with some naïve Christians espousing atheists' or agnostics' inherent right to believe or not believe. (Clearly, in America, citizens have such a "right.") Nevertheless, the Christian movement rests on "making disciples" in the name of our Savior, Jesus Christ. More than mere coexistence with others, sincere Christians aim to bring others to the Christian worldview. In a word, we should actively aim to bring forth new converts for the kingdom of God!

Those thirty years, moreover, were characterized by an obvious attempt to seize new territory for God (in seeing increasing numbers of people embracing the Christian faith). As a very young pastor (starting at twenty-two years old), I recognized my need for additional training. I attended a week-long "School of Evangelism," sponsored by the Billy Graham Evangelistic Association. We learned to prioritize evangelism for local congregations. With unbridled enthusiasm for capturing the lost, I took the materials home to my congregation. Sadly, my passion was doused. I quickly discovered that they valued institutional maintenance over reaching the lost. Interestingly, I have never attended another evangelism school of its kind since, not because I lost interest in the subject; but because of the scarcity of such conferences amid new Christian concerns.

Further, my own library of books on Christian evangelism dates from the 1970s through the '90s: *Master Plan of Evangelism* by Robert Coleman; *Out of the Salt-shaker, into the World* by Rebecca Pippert; *Making Friends for Christ* by Wayne McDill; *How to Give Away Your Faith* by Paul Little; *Out of the Comfort Zone* by Ray Comfort; *Evangelism and the Sovereignty of God* by J. I. Packer; *The Church as Evangelist* by George Sweazay; *Leading Your Church in Evangelism* by Lewis Drummond; *The Divine Art of Soul-winning* by J. Oswald Sanders; *Every Member Evangelism for Today* by Fish and Conant; *Concentric Circles of Concern* by W. Oscar Thompson, among others.

Interestingly, over the last 20 years, I have few, if any, books written specifically on evangelism, the preeminent calling of Christianity.

Moreover, in my home denomination, the National Baptist Convention, USA, Inc., arguably the largest seminar for ministers, was dedicated to evangelism, and led by the late Dr. Manuel L. Scott Sr. It attracted thousands of ministers, with a singular appeal designed to influence their congregations in reaching the lost for salvation through Christ. That evangelism seminar lasted until the new century, 2000, coinciding with Dr. Scott's declining health.

Whatever happened to our calling from God to serve as *"salt"* (Matthew 5:13) in a bland, dispirited, vapid culture?

Whatever happened to our sense of Christians as *"light"* (Matthew 5:14) in a world where millions grope in darkness, wallowing in sinful confusion?

Whatever happened to the righteous in Christ being that *"city"* (Matthew 5:14b) perched on a hill, giving direction to a worn, wounded, wondering world?

Whatever happened to God's people, redeemed by Christ, serving as *"ambassadors"* (2 Corinthians 5:20), negotiating the terms by which fellowship with the heavenly Father can be established?

In short, whatever happened to Christian evangelism?

I ask these questions because I am hurt by the lack of national Christian leaders and Christian congregations leading on this critical issue. Perhaps I can make the point better by referencing this statement from a colleague: "I have been in this Christian group for many years. Three presidents have served it; and I have yet to hear any one of them call for direct Christian evangelism."

The problem of de-emphasizing evangelism, what should be our preeminent calling, means Christian leaders, denominations, congregations and individuals often engage in useful activities without interacting with the targeted audience of Christ: *"For the Son of Man has come to seek and to save that which was lost"* (Luke 19:10). Indeed, Christ's religious detractors (see Matthew, Chapters 22 and 23) accused Him of being too cozy with prostitutes, men and women of questionable character, tax collectors, fishermen, political zealots, diseased people, the poor, the marginalized and others of their ilk.

The early twenty-first-century world exposes many spiritual, economic, social, demographic, personal, and cultural shifts, which all conspire to shape Christian perspectives. Within our nation and globally, important voices are raised in the Christian family. While many Christian congregations reach the "megachurch" level, we yearn for influential leaders to sound the alarm for evangelistic engagement by Christians on a large scale.

At the same time, in the secular environment, the last decade has been shaped by innumerable challenges: 9/11 events, two unpopular wars (in Iraq and Afghanistan), a housing crisis, economic uncertainty, the historic election of the first black US president, immigration debates, high unemployment, widening income inequality, gun-control battles, educational reform, the rise of so-called same-sex marriages, health-care reform, legalized medical marijuana, Tea Party extremism questioning the size and scope of government, the ubiquity of social media, maddening technological advances, and other moral, social, and political issues. If the Christian church fails to respond to these challenges with biblical and moral precepts, lost humanity wonders as to Christian compassion and interest in their daily struggles. Indeed, when God's people offer insight and wisdom from a caring Christian perspective, we enhance evangelistic effectiveness and engagement.

Critically, the agenda of those setting the terms of Christian engagement seems to involve saved, holy, middle-class, worshipful, prayerful, pious, prosperous, victorious living, without overt concern for the lost among us. Consider the fact that national Christian conferences have as their themes those enumerated emphases, along with "empowerment," and "next level." Christian leaders and congregations yearn to obtain principles of spiritual, personal, numerical, financial, and material growth, without advancing the kingdom of God through conversions of the lost!

Too often, in my judgment, Christian leaders and their congregations are too concerned with several objectives: budgets, buildings, prosperity, prominence and local influence. In the process, too many have lost their focus. Sunday worship (what many call "service"), has shifted the focus away from the lost. Baptisms are not pursued nor celebrated; numerical growth is measured more by disaffected parishioners moving from one Christian congregation to another one, rather than new converts. When saints of God fail to invite the lost to salvation through Christ, or often, even to attend worship, it should not surprise Christian leaders when there is a drop-off in Christian vibrancy. No congregation, whatever its size, can function as Christ designed the Christian fellowship without infusions of new people, asking new questions and bringing new life situations.

Christian churches (and Christian denominations, for that matter) lose their "electricity" and spiritual dynamism when they fail to attract new adherents. Again, Christianity today represents a movement of converted, transformed, born-again, Christ-exalting, Holy Spirit-led, Word-centered people, coming together to form the body of Christ.

If we look to theological academies for leadership in Christian evangelism, in the main, they too fail us. Such institutions (I am a product of two esteemed, accredited, well-known ones) serve to polish students in areas such as church history, biblical languages, Christian administration, systematic theology, missiology, hermeneutics, and homiletics. For the most part, they prepare students for missionary work, para-church leadership, non-profit involvement, academy teaching, and serving as senior pastors and workers in local congregations. Again, Christianity continues its "maintenance" thrust, rather than deliberate outreach, seeking the unsaved in our communities, cities, and states across America, and globally.

While Christian evangelism has never been completely eradicated from the agenda in American congregational life, a new phenomenon swept the body of Christ, starting in the late 1970s, with implications all the way to the present moment.

The Word of Faith movement added a new dimension to the discussion of what constitutes Christian truth and mission. Leaders and congregations were part of a global Charismatic Awakening.

Part of their appeal were beliefs and teachings which held that, along with the deity and vicarious death, resurrection, and ascension of Christ, in this new period, God wanted to materially bless and literally prosper those who proclaimed, relied upon, and acted in "faith." (Now, we must concede that every insightful Bible student affirms the fundamental reality of Hebrews 11, a chapter dedicated to God's exploits through people of faith.) Thus, through a synthesis of Neo-Pentecostalism, based on a critical biblical concept (faith), a world-wide movement was launched.

Moreover, against a staid, tradition-based, inert Christian system, the Word of Faith movement declared the vibrancy and dynamism of the Holy Spirit of God at work in the Christian family. Its worship music was alive, praise-oriented, uplifting, conveying the power of God to the individual saint of God. Its leaders— clad in business suits and in some cases, casual attire rather than clerical vestments—reminded saints of the importance of biblical teaching, unleashing a torrent of biblical verses to consider, exhorting believers to open their Bibles, to underline, and to take notes, all to enhance the intake of the Word of God. Among African-American Christians of all denominational stripes, emotional, dramatic, rhetorical, methodical, musical, celebrative preaching became passé and outmoded. Enlightened, middle-class, bourgeois, striving, professional blacks would no longer tolerate "old-time" worship practices or teachings. Initially, these blacks flocked to white congregations; later, they started their own congregations, to great acclaim!

In regards to evangelism, as I view it, this movement made Christianity much more personal and insular, as the near fixation became "my praise," my worship," "my deliverance," "my marriage," "my healing," and "my prosperity," without sufficient regard for the salvation of the lost. Large ministries were started in suburban areas, as African Americans and others were attracted to a spiritual philosophy emphasizing all Christians could *get from God* (innumerable benefits), without the concomitant demand of what Christians should *do for God* (evangelize an unsaved world with the message of Christ).

Without question, this new movement brought much benefit to the body of Christ, by way of new emphases (nomenclature, spiritual gifts, celebration of the Holy Spirit, enhancement of the Word, dynamism in worship, emphasis on holiness). Yet, at the same time, it and other trends caused more Christians to emphasize "cleaning" saved fish, rather than "catching" lost ones.

For the last 40 years in America, then, in various ways, the Christian family has turned inward, focused on our needs, in the process forsaking the "net" of divine grace and eternal love from above. Through large worship gatherings, teaching tapes, well-written books, national conferences and more, Christians wash and mend their "nets" (Luke 5:2b), not expecting to attract unsaved "fish" to the kingdom of God.

Much of the phenomenal numerical growth of these new congregations ("Christian centers") stems from disaffected saints who moved their allegiance and support from traditional congregations. The message of God's capacity and willingness, on the basis of faith, to grant prosperity to antsy and impatient strivers took hold in many hearts and minds. The quick route to fulfillment and material gain ("Claim your blessings!"), primarily to lower-income people, proved irresistible.

To be sure, unsaved people were attracted to Christian congregations whose primary teachings required little of them besides a short, spirited worship and living a godly existence (fleshly avoidance), while asking God for untold treasures. If, on the other hand, the unsaved were presented with stark truths from the entire Word, it would include the following: God meets those who sacrifice, who strain, and who struggle, who really exert themselves for a quality education, who marshal their resources, who defer their gratification, who commit to marriage, who provide for their children. In fact, not all saints will prosper, because many are not disciplined enough. Further, God blesses on the basis of grace more than merit. And, God honors those who work long, hard and creatively. He then expects the saved to lead others to life transformation through Christ. Now, that biblical, pragmatic, tough message may not resonate as well!

Rather than an ecclesiological club with sublime benefits accruing to members, the Christian movement must again see herself as a refuge for the empty, a haven for those in need of spiritual guidance, comfort in life's storm, especially for millions disconnected from true living, which can only be found in a relationship with God, made possible through His Son and our Savior.

Evangelistic success with the lost, as I view it, hinges on saints of God being real, transparent, and focused on the challenges of everyday living. Christians watch the same news channels as the unsaved, while discerning deeper insight; we watch secular movies, knowing there are more fundamental ways to real "life"; we need health-care insurance, even as God serves as ultimate

Healer; we are impacted by the same economy, though we know the true Source of our needs; we follow the same societal rules, even as we affirm a higher, biblical ethic and value system; we require secular employment, even as God provides for our needs; we vote in elections because we are citizens, even as we note inherent corruption in the electoral process; we are inundated by the same weather, even as we look to God to guide us through it. An older generation of saints captured this realty thusly: "Christians are *in* the world, but not *of* the world." And, amidst inevitable trials, they counseled: "God rains on the just and the unjust."

Knowing that, in too many cases, the Christian church has strayed from its calling to evangelize the lost, I must mention the way back to our "north star." We must rekindle the fire of evangelism, seeking the salvation of all, knowing that the blood of Jesus reaches from the lowest valley to the highest mountain. Persons of every class, creed, condition, ethnicity, gender, and orientation are welcome to the throne of grace, where Christ pleads our case before the heavenly Father: *"Therefore, being justified by faith, we have peace with God through our Lord Jesus Christ"* (Romans 5:1).

While many move away from overt appeals to the lost, I am more convinced than ever that the real dynamic for Christian living lies in renewed enthusiasm for taking the gospel message out of the Christian sanctuary, and placing it firmly in the hearts of those moving through the secular streets. Indeed, Christians need to recognize the sobering consequences for the lost among us (eternal separation from God), and the challenges of living unsaved today (a post-modern worldview). What we need most, nevertheless, are the strong voices of Christian leaders, despite their being busy, fractured by innumerable concerns, ensconced in ecclesiological satisfaction, or just plain laziness. They are the keys to Christian evangelism engagement. Accordingly, I challenge Christian leaders to preach, teach, train, model and celebrate the potential of new converts to the Christian faith, epitomizing advancement of the kingdom of God.

If Christian leaders and congregants truly recognize the severity of our times in present-day America with falling morals, rampant abuse, murder, corruption, family dysfunction, violence, drug abuse, depravity, political gridlock, ingrained poverty, and a general drift, we will redouble our efforts to reach those enmeshed in sin, languishing in defeat, far from the peaceful shore in Christ. Too many around us are stained with personal shame, aiming to elude internal guilt, yet unsure of the best means of coping with their myriad challenges.

The Gospel of Jesus Christ still represents the central remedy for all that ails humanity, irrespective of titles, achievements, status, plaudits, and more. When people are "sin-sick," everything else pales in comparison: *"For what will a man be profited, if he gains the whole world, and forfeits his soul? Or what will a man give in exchange for his soul?"* (Matthew 16:26).

Since individuals are too valuable to waste, retaining the image of God, though soiled and sullied in the fall, we must deploy ourselves to the fields of the lost, the hurting, the broken, the ignored, and the unwanted.

Christians can recover their urgency for Christian evangelism, provided we recognize the depth of depravity and despair lost people live with every day. Under the veneer of material benefits (cash, clothes, cars, boats, vacations, stocks, bonds, mutual funds, elaborate plans), so many try to discover joy and lasting significance. Unfortunately, *Forbes Magazine's* wealthy (athletes, entertainers, private-equity managers, hedge-fund leaders, corporate CEOs, philanthropists, and others) cannot assuage a guilty conscience, nor ease the pain of emptiness in the human heart. That vacuum of hope can only—I repeat only!—be filled by the Master, the Lord Jesus Christ.

And, such news must be shared with a lost world of humanity, as never before.

Whatever happened to Christian evangelism (lack of leaders, new emphases on "faith," and privatized devotion to God), reminds us of the importance of each saint of God reaching another, with the news of Christ's salvation.

CHAPTER 2

Present-day Christian Concerns

It is a dichotomy long dominant in Christian circles, but really apparent in present-day Christendom: *"What represents the proper balance between concern for building up the saved over against actively seeking the unsaved, the lost?"* In other words, should the Christian witness primarily concern itself with "cleaning" fish, while avoiding the Christ-ordained mission and responsibility of "catching" fish?

Nationally, there are prominent Christian leaders noted for their ability to "clean" saved fish: teaching, preaching, seminars, conferences, books, television appearances, magazine covers, and more attest to their propensity. Such leaders emphasize worship, prayer, sacrifice, marriage, holiness, and the like as absolute "musts" for all who would exemplify Christ. Within their public proclamation of the Word, however, they fail to challenge Christians, as they coddle saints in a cocoon of comfort: "Saint of God, obtain your healing, your breakthrough, your deliverance, your prosperity, strengthen your marriage, and more."

As a mature Christian leader (thirty-one years as a pastor), I am troubled, because seldom do such prominent voices use their spiritual influence to issue a clarion call for active, engaged soul-winners. In my view, too many fail to challenge saints in Christ's mission to lead others to the knowledge of the Savior. When God gives leaders a "large microphone," (large congregation, national television audience, conference hosting, etc.), they must use it for godly ends, rather than small agendas, serving only those already affiliated with Christ.

I hold that the Christian witness today—in its diversity, in its geographic dominance in America, in its financial heft, in its attempt to capture wider attention—has lost sight of its mission. Too often, Christians don't know why we exist. If we asked thousands of Christian saints, "What is the Christian mission?" many would be clueless. After stammering somewhat, most would probably confine that mission to the Sunday sanctuary.

Many believe the Christian mission involves worship, preaching, teaching, and prayer, helping the saved live better, more focused, godly, prayerful lives. Sadly, it would stop there. I believe, however, that there is much more to the Christian mission.

Let me clarify this point better: As a "seasoned" Christian pastor, I know that part of my God-ordained task involves the command, *"Feed my sheep"* (John 21:15-17). Also, I am aware of the Word: *"...shepherding the flock of God among you, exercising oversight not under compulsion, but voluntarily, according to the will of God; and not for sordid gain, but with eagerness; nor yet as lording it over those allotted to your charge, but proving to be examples to the flock. And when the Chief Shepherd appears, you will receive the unfailing crown of glory"* (1 Peter 5:2-4). Thus, every Lord's Day I relish the opportunity to open the Word of God, to nurture saints in the mysteries of God, to stand with them through major challenges, and to watch them flourish in the supernatural realm.

All I aim for in Christian ministry is geared toward producing godly, maturing, prayerful, obedient, discerning, Word-centered, Christ-exalting, Spirit-directed Christian disciples. While that objective defines me, I want to achieve more: leading unsaved people to the Savior.

Before the people of God, however, I find myself hoping, really praying, that they will grow in Christ in such ways they then will help others know of the Savior. It just seems wasteful to me: millions of saints in America worshipping Sunday after Sunday, rapturous in joy, while millions more are unsaved, languishing in sin, guilt, and shame. Does anyone really care about the lost? I do, and I pray that you do.

I sense in our rush to demonstrate daily holiness that many Christian leaders and congregations are renowned as oases for teaching the Bible, extolling its virtues, living sanctified lives, growing in the faith, and claiming the promises of prosperity; yet, many are blithely disconnected from the unsaved in our midst. That stance, unfortunately, takes the Christian witness away from its core mission: bringing new people to saving faith in Christ.

If preaching and teaching the Word should have an objective (and they should), how do we measure progress in worship, in holiness, in prayerfulness, in tithing, in developing Christian character, and so many other valuable spiritual themes? Yet, we persist in plugging away at such themes.

On the other hand, if we emphasize Christian evangelism, the one who truly catches its relevance will lead a soul to Christ. It's that simple! A new convert, then, represents tangible, empirical, verifiable witness to having believed the message. By that measure, how many are really "locked-in" to the Gospel?

We need to grapple with this matter of *"balance."* Unless we reach a consensus as to where to plant the Christian flag of engagement, the Christian witness will be hampered in its national and global effectiveness. Currently, with every imaginable tool at our disposal, the Christian witness seems paralyzed before a world system that views Christianity and Christians as quaint, but not vital to their life perspective, or their value system. Morally, Christians are confused; ethically, we are challenged; politically, we are duped; economically, we are dwarfed; intellectually, we forfeit the debate; and influentially, we are marginal, at best.

In one area, however, we have unparalleled influence over this world's system: Christians know the only Source of grace, sustenance, purpose and real life. We know an awesome, loving heavenly Father, keenly interested in humanity created in His image. We know Jesus Christ, the all-sufficient Savior, sent by God to redeem fallen humanity. We know that the Cross of Calvary triumphs over death, hell and the grave. We know the regenerating power of the Holy Spirit, who yet convicts lost, unsaved, un-regenerate persons. We know the Word of God—inerrant, infallible, inexhaustible, and authoritative—as it establishes principles for successful living.

The word *Balance* means that Christians worship and engage in learning; that we share evangelism and discipleship. Christian leaders also know their job description: *"He gave some as ... pastors and teachers, for the equipping of the saints for the work of service, to the building up of the body of Christ..."* (Ephesians 4:11-12). Equipping saints represents an arduous, time-consuming ministry of teaching, led by the pastor. Most often, it cannot be fully accomplished on Sunday mornings. Instead, teaching (particularly on Christian evangelism) must be done throughout the week by the spiritual leader, as well as by other leaders in the fellowship. If no Bible teaching occurs, nothing changes!

As Ephesians 4:12 (quoted earlier) admonishes, pastoral leaders "equip the saints" by furnishing tools (biblical, spiritual, relational, intellectual, practical) necessary for sharing Christ as Savior with lost friends, family members, neighbors, co-workers, acquaintances, and others. The pastoral role in evangelism teaching/training resembles that of a coach, offering guidance to players, all of whom possess different skill levels, athleticism and natural abilities; though all must execute plays within a "game-plan." In this regard, several relevant Scriptures (Romans 3:23; 5:8; 6:23; 8:1; 10:9-10) form the "game-plan" for reaching the unsaved masses.

When God's revelation of grace through Christ is shared through the power of the Holy Spirit, saints can expect divine results. So, people should come to salvation and new life when Christ is exalted: *"And I, if I be lifted up from the earth, will draw all men to Myself"* (John 12:32).

In my youth, I recall African-American ministers of an earlier generation saying, *"The great mistake His enemies made was to lift Jesus on the Cross, for when they did so, it led to miraculous consequences."* They argued that, once He was lifted up, the thief on the Cross was promised eternity with the Savior; the centurion soldier affirmed Him as the Son of God; and the earth was awash in darkness for three hours (Luke 23:33-47). Then, they brought the concept of the lifted Christ to the present day, celebrating Him as their personal Savior! For today, we need such stark, imaginative, Bible-based preaching again, if sinners are to be converted to Christ.

Knowing that the elevated Savior possesses ultimate "drawing power" takes the responsibility off the shoulders of Christian leaders, no matter their scholarship, creativity, charisma, eloquence, wit or personality. Let this generation hear it anew: Christ draws people to the kingdom of God. He does use people, but, ultimately, He draws!

Indeed, what I encourage, Christian evangelism teaching, if done consistently, founded on the Word of God, in the power of the Holy Spirit, eventually establishes a culture within that church fellowship. Congregants begin to share Christ with the unsaved as the normative experience of their lives. They make the most of every opportunity to express the joy of their existence. Evangelizing others becomes almost automatic. While some people will continually express pessimism, anxiety, frustration, or speculation, well-taught, evangelism-immersed saints of God will speak faith in God, celebrating Christ's forgiveness. Proudly, such saints will plead "Guilty" to a charge of being captivated by the wonders of God's grace, unable to converse with others before raising the "main matter": "Are you saved?"

My late mentor, Dr. Edward V. Hill of Los Angeles and world acclaim, used to remind younger clergy: *"Christian leaders must determine whether they will be keepers of the aquarium, or 'fishers of men.' The choice will dictate your ministry effectiveness."*

"Keeping the aquarium" means engagement in everyday leadership chores: visiting the sick, counseling, leading worship, preaching a sermon, attending church meetings, marrying couples and other vital works which often amount to "maintenance" ministry. Clearly, today, with anemic ministries across the landscape, with few baptisms, and few new faces in worship, we have many leaders adept at "keeping the aquarium."

Among many things, "keeping the aquarium" means: maintaining a low profile, not upsetting anything, just enjoying a regular paycheck for an unfocused, befuddled, lazy Christian leader. That type of leader also "fits" in a Christian congregation known for lofty history, vaunted tradition, and high standing in the community. Yet, absent concern for the lost, the very heart, core, and pulse of that fellowship are missing. Not long afterward, that fellowship will become a relic, a has-been, an irrelevant footnote to what God could have done: *"O Jerusalem, Jerusalem...How often I wanted to gather your children together, the way a hen gathers her chicks under her wings, and you were unwilling. Behold, your house is being left to you desolate!"* (Matthew 23:37).

In my judgment, Christian leaders and congregations must periodically examine themselves: *"Are we seeing new people come to Christ through our fellowship?"* *"When was the last time we celebrated some baptisms?"* *"Are we intentionally reaching out to the unsaved?"* *"How many unsaved and un-churched visitors came to worship last Sunday?"* These are diagnostic questions for a Christian fellowship sensitive to the Master's mission: *to seek and to save the lost* (Luke 19:10).

Notice among the questions cited above, none inquired as to building size, annual budget, governing structure, denominational ties, prominent members, pastoral influence, or other ephemeral matters. Instead, the Christian witness exists to glorify God, exalt Christ, obey Scripture, and grow in Him, while advancing the kingdom of God through new souls led to Christ, in the process transforming society. Please carefully re-read that last sentence.

As a Christian leader, I need to ask: Is your church living up to that biblical standard? Or, as a congregant, if the Christian fellowship you regularly attend does not reach up to that ideal, please ask God if you should leave there, immediately. Led by Him, find a Christian fellowship where such is the spiritual order.

Something strange occurs within a Christian fellowship when unsaved persons don't come forward, seeking salvation in Christ. That fellowship mimics a science-fiction movie, with red-eyed zombies walking about. Sundays become rote "services," (not "worships") devoid of life, as real life begins with conversions to Christ. Choirs sing of the great power of God, but when there are few candidates for baptism, that congregation becomes, switching metaphors, like a hospital with a morgue but not a maternity ward.

The key notion I assert here is "balance": promote saints' growth in Christ, while challenging them to bring new persons to salvation through Christ. As with most New Testament concepts, the apostle Paul strikes the proper balance: Christian evangelism and Christian nurture; fishing and cleaning; teaching and soul-winning. If we fail in the former, the latter will inevitably be feckless, insipid and stale. Question: Is your ministry a balanced one?

If the Christian church is composed of born-again, converted, transformed, blood-washed, followers of Christ (and, it is), we must share His passion for lost souls. The passion must transcend mere words, forming an action agenda, taking saints into direct contact with unsaved friends, family members, neighbors, co-workers and people in general.

My other thesis holds that, because they are made in His image and according to His likeness, people really matter to God. All kinds of people matter: intelligent people, illiterate people, broken people, marginalized people, high-class people, middle-class people, low-class people, no-class people, introverted people, gregarious people, mean people, engaging people, guilt-ridden people, shame-filled people, black people, white people, brown people, yellow people, red people. By now it should be abundantly clear: God loves and extends mercy and grace to all kinds of people! Note the Scripture: *"And seeing the multitudes, He felt compassion for them, because they were distressed and downcast like sheep without a shepherd"* (Matthew 9:36). The love of God, as well as the human condition, has not changed!

Further, when the average American congregation remains stuck somewhere below 100 regular attendees each Lord's Day, irrespective of denomination, race/ethnicity, locale, status or income, while millions populate urban settings, there is, indeed, no "sinner shortage" (another Dr. Hill saying!). Instead, we need courageous, creative, dynamic, determined, godly Christian leaders, who will fervently appeal for saints of God, willing to deploy as "soul-winners."

Deployment is more than pious words. Deployment represents intentional, concerted action, meaning to really do it. The Nike ad says it best: "Just do it." I am thus raising my voice, whenever Christians gather, saying, "Come, on, church, let's evangelize the unsaved."

What hinders present-day evangelistic engagement is the faulty notion of seeing few results, despite a great deal of trying. Many Christian leaders feel Peter's pain, as he said to the Lord Jesus: *"Master, we worked hard all night and caught nothing, but at Your bidding I will let down the nets"* (Luke 5:5). Please catch (pun intended!) the over-arching spiritual lesson: previous failure does not guarantee a present one. Rather, it prepares us for stupendous success, as Peter and his companions *"enclosed a great quantity of fish; and their nets began to break"* (Luke 5:6).

Regarding the matter of failure, consider the work of a car salesman. Perhaps he has a poor day of sales: many "lookers," but few actual purchasers. I hope he will not quit the business because of one day's lack of success. Likewise, the Christian leader and congregation must not give up on the unsaved, simply because no one came to Christ last Sunday. Instead, use that lack of tangible results as motivation and inspiration for next Sunday's anticipated "harvest."

Our prayers to God for wisdom in any undertaking, especially evangelism, should be supplemented by practical engagement. In other words, prayer and planning are critical for progress. So, once we arise from our knees, we must turn our heels toward those languishing in guilt and shame, unable to change their spiritual condition. Find the unsaved, and present them with the Christ message.

I will repeat a theme shared elsewhere in this book: strangely, instead of *"Going,"* Christians expect the lost to, somehow, *"Come."*

The barometer for Christian effectiveness should be represented by tangible conversions, bringing persons from darkness to the light of Christ. Yet, many Christian congregations go weeks, or months, without a new convert being produced. While that fact is not surprising, the greater fact is no one in that congregation seems overly bothered by no new "fish!"

In many cases, Christian leaders and congregants content themselves with feeble justifications for lack of conversions: *"When we reach unity in Christ, being on "one accord," then, God will produce results."* Or, *"When we pray more fervently, God will bless us with new converts."* Or, *"If we enhance the children's ministry, the music ministry, the facility, then, God will send new people."* My analysis of those sentiments (unity, prayer, ministries and facilities) is that, too often, saints put the responsibility on God, and on extraneous matters, rather than accepting their role in sharing the pulsating, compelling, life-affirming message of Christ with the unsaved.

If one has read the Scripture, one knows what really pleases God: *"There will be more joy in heaven over one sinner who repents than over ninety-nine righteous persons who need no repentance"* (Luke 15:7, 10). So, successful worship involves sinners coming to repentance. Christians only make inroads into the enemies' camp when, by the Spirit's power, we liberate spiritual captives. Simply enjoying personal salvation, while focusing on the deficiencies of the saved, will never "move-the-needle."

I would submit to all, that the Christian church is actually "out-of-balance": too much sanctuary, not enough streets. Put differently, too much church work, not enough Christ work. Indeed, Christ work represents seeking the lost (Luke 19:10).

None of what presently ails God's church—lack of mission, feeble anointing by God's Spirit, weak biblical exposition, few new converts, leadership scandals, financial impropriety, infrequent divine manifestations, etc. - should inhibit our fervor. The attacks of the enemy are subtle, though, over time, quite devastating. Doing nothing is one of his best strategies to limit God's kingdom advance. Yet, through energetic evangelism, we can know and do better!

Several hurdles hinder personal evangelism (fear, laziness, busy lives, expectation of failure, not knowing Scripture, not knowing unsaved people, etc.). In fact, Christ works through yielded saints: *"Now to Him who is able to do exceeding abundantly beyond all that we ask or think, according to the power that works within us"* (Ephesians 3:20). While we trust, Christ works, not according to our power, but according to His.

Something mysterious, marvelous, and glorious occurs when saints open their mouths in evangelistic engagement: God takes our fearlessness and uses us as instruments of insight, whereby the unsaved get to know of God's love and grace in Christ. If saints today were left with only one verse of Scripture to define God's grace, it would be sufficient for humanity's salvation: *"For God so loved the world, that He gave His only begotten Son, that whoever believes in Him should not perish, but have eternal life"* (John 3:16).

While that verse is, arguably, the most well-known one in the Bible, it should not be neglected in conveying the depths of divine grace for lost humanity. Note its pulsating, salient, definitive truths: *"God so loved,"* *"the world,"* *"He gave,"* *"His only begotten Son,"* *"whoever,"* *"believes in Him,"* *"shall not perish,"* for the promise entails *"eternal life."* These italicized phrases and words could form the basis of meaningful books on evangelism. In brief, however, they tell of a gracious God, offering salvation to all who will trust His Son as sole sacrifice for personal sin.

Thus, Christian evangelism means we tell the story of God's love in Christ...and then, tell it again...and again!

Finally, we dispel a Christian witness too inward-focused, by admonishing, teaching, training, pushing, prodding, goading, and challenging God's redeemed to return to their highest priority: reaching the lost. That Christ-based message, in my judgment, has been eclipsed by many good Christian causes (worship, prayer, Bible content, holiness, taking authority, material blessings/prosperity, and social justice). Indeed, pursuit of the good has supplanted passion for the great. In Revelation 2:4, God indicted His church: *"But I have this against you, that you have left your first love."* Incredibly, this Ephesian fellowship, commended 30 years before, had now intentionally forsaken its calling to represent Christ before the unsaved.

If present-day followers of Christ turn from seeking the lost to obsessing over trivialities (leaders, buildings, budgets, blessings, tradition, irrelevant issues), we should expect God's instruction: *"Do the deeds you did at first"* (Revelation 2:5). In short, God says something profound: Get back to the basic cornerstones of constructive engagement (evangelism, soul-winning, bringing new converts, adding persons to the kingdom of God).

Increasingly, American youth are chafing under stultifying images of a Christian Church intent on maintenance rather than structural change. Youthful rebellion takes the form of nihilism, hedonism, and serious questioning of the moral integrity of Christianity over the last 30-plus years. Manifestations of that rebellion include desire for up-tempo music, shorter worships, and "fun" encounters.

Other Christian youth, against principles from the Word of God, have adopted popular trends of the world: tattoos, body piercing, cursing, promiscuity, embracing and "alternative lifestyles." Sociologists term this the "post-modern" generation. Perhaps, wiser, mature saints of God might begin their evangelistic outreach among children and grandchildren, as more have become enamored and attracted to an unsaved, amoral, helter-skelter worldview.

I implore Christian leaders, in hoping to shape Christian outreach in the next decades: we must recognize the shifting demographic of America. More and more persons are in a younger cohort: ages 18 through 40. They want relevance in Christianity, clear moral/ethical guidelines, ways to integrate technology into their relationships, centered in Christ, with a strong sense of practical application of the Word of God. As the ad tag-line suggests, with an alteration: "This must not be your grandfather's Christianity."

My Louisville, Kentucky colleague in Christ, Dr. Kevin Cosby, reminds the Christian witness that change is good, necessary, and inevitable. He reasons: "Aunt Jemima on the syrup bottle sports a new hairdo, garments and an enhanced smile." Therein is our present challenge: "tweak" the method (evangelism), while maintaining the message (Christ). As we aim to chart our future course, we must ensure that nothing saps the church of her strength: the name of our Savior, Jesus Christ.

I contend that, in viewing the contemporary Christian scene, too many Christian leaders and saints of God are stagnating due to cowardice, which becomes the master of moral indignation. In hearing me speak, and reading my words, many sense my frustration with "do-nothing" Christianity, cloistered in the sanctuary, rather than taking it into the streets. My passion often overwhelms me, as I truly want to see the world come to salvation through Christ. This global objective does not emerge from my head, but rather it comes from my close reading of the heartbeat of our Savior: *"For the Son of Man has come to seek and to save that which was lost"* (Luke 19:10).

To further polish the point, allow me to go on. Christian leaders not passionate regarding reaching the unsaved greatly concern me. I cannot fathom their view of Christianity. Christian congregations not concerned with the lost bore and sicken me! Whole Christian denominations not organized and not faithfully articulating an agenda based in evangelism do not deserve emotional, financial, or moral support of constituent congregations. That position places me firmly in the camp of an outsider, to which I gladly plead, "Guilty." Change driven by dynamic evangelism must awaken a "sleeping giant," otherwise known as the church of the Lord Jesus Christ.

Every Christian congregation in America (and globally) would be revolutionized for God and for good by an infusion of new converts to Christ. They would bring ideas, concepts, questions, longings, doubts, yearnings, questions, methods, often disturbing the comfort of many entrenched saints. Yet, their presence might cause the old guard to rethink its assumptions regarding what is acceptable in the kingdom of God. In fact, we might discern that some of our traditional ways have been antithetical to the forward movement of the Christian witness, keeping us small and irrelevant in the eyes of millions.

None can even imagine what the Church would look like with multiple baptisms occurring each Lord's Day. I assert it would bring a sense of unbridled expectancy in Christ. On a desert road, after hearing the presentation of the gospel of Christ, an Ethiopian eunuch captures the tone of which I speak: *"Look! Water! What prevents me from being baptized?"* (Acts 8:36). That enthusiasm following a "right-now" encounter with Christ would enhance any Christian fellowship. Let more of us pray that God will "trouble the waters," after many have been led to saving faith in Christ by our personal evangelism, our intentional soul-winning.

If, on the other hand, we grant that the enemy seeks to immobilize vast swaths of the Christian witness through indifference, at least a few should vow: "I aim to go down fighting." We should refuse to forfeit the "game," even as we admit the seeming futility of many current efforts by Christian leaders and congregations.

Instead, I liken our present plight to an athletic event, say, a basketball game. Our team is behind, with the clock ticking. Yet, we still have the ball in our possession! That means, in the name of Christ, more of us must shoot it!

Christians "shoot" in referencing the grace of God in all of our lives.

Christians "shoot" by calling humanity to repentance.

Christians "shoot" by praying for and working toward millions of conversions.

Christians "shoot" when we worship God, "in spirit and in truth."

Christians "shoot" as we invite people to the knowledge of Christ.

Christians "shoot" when we call utmost attention to that hill called Calvary!

Christians "shoot" in a unique invitation to discipleship: clear, simple, and profound.

And, not surprisingly, saints can only win when they "shoot the ball." Indeed, in varying ways, I yearn to hear of and witness countless "victories" in the name of Jesus Christ! After all, saints of God are *"more than conquerors"* through Christ (Romans 8:37). With winning assured by God, let the contest continue!

Join me, then, in destroying Christianity dedicated to relishing the status-quo. In its place, help me revive the Church of Jesus Christ, obedient to Christ's mandate, by deploying saints to the unsaved.

CHAPTER 3

Capturing Christ's Evangelistic Agenda

Rather than viewing Christian evangelism as some great idea of Christian leaders—historical or contemporary—hoping to generate new members, to fill worship spaces, we must view the matter as a completely divine imperative. Lovingly informing persons of ultimate hope in Christ represents, then, a grand, gracious idea. Further, that one's life can be radically and eternally transformed by Christ involves nothing less than a divine ideal. Christian evangelism, then, implicates all dedicated, sincere, committed followers of Christ in carrying it out. Christ's command in Acts 1:8 (*"you shall be My witnesses..."*) means world evangelism of humanity. Indeed, His words there are, in fact, a binding imperative, over against a practical suggestion!

Put differently, Christian evangelism involves the apex of the God idea, given expression by the Lord Jesus Christ. In the Gospel of Matthew, Chapter 16, our Savior elicits answers to His identity from the perspective of the masses who have heard of Him. News of Him has by now spread across various geographical areas. As His earthly ministry takes shape, and as it fills hearts and minds, Christ asks the disciples to gauge peoples' responses. Famously, Peter declares transcendent truth: *"Thou art the Christ, the Son of the living God"* (Matthew 16:16).

For all times, that statement captures the essence of genuine faith in the Savior of the world. It forms the basis for establishing a dedicated, unique group called the "Church of the Lord Jesus Christ." Yet, a few verses later, Christ rebuked Peter because Peter sought to dissuade Christ from His ultimate mission: dying for humanity, then being raised by God on the third day. Hear the poignant words of the One resolute in His mission: *"Get behind Me, Satan! You are a stumbling block to Me; for you are not setting your mind on God's interests, but man's"* (Matthew 16:23).

Consider it: in the space of seven verses, Peter went from the thrill of accurately identifying the Master to the agony of seeking to thwart His mission. How could this be? Perhaps, Peter wanted (along with many of us today) salvation for ourselves and others, without the gory, gloomy Cross. Maybe today we want a positive, affirming, uplifting message, when, in truth, the Christian message talks of liberation from "sin," calling for "repentance," "faith," and "acceptance of Christ." Indeed, God's interest is quite clear, and greater than humanity's plan: the redemption of humanity, ending alienation for those tainted by the fall of humanity. Deterioration in fellowship between God and humanity stretches all the way back to our original parents, Adam and Eve. Similarly, the highest ethic today involves establishing the parameters for a successful relationship with our heavenly Father: necessarily, it flows through His Son, Jesus Christ. Thus, we are presented with the non-negotiable truth upon which all of life rests.

In his defense, part of what drove Peter's rebuke of Christ, arguing against His impending death was a serious misinterpretation of the Savior's reason for coming to earth in the first place. While Christ did, in fact, teach moral and ethical principles, this was not the primary purpose of His coming. While He did perform multiple physical miracles for injured, broken, and diseased people, this, again, did not entail His primary purpose. Finally, while He did engage minds through parables, this, too, did not capture His essential work given by God.

The primary purpose of Christ's coming to the earth realm was twofold, as the Matthew 16:21ff text demonstrates: 1) To die for humanity's sin; and 2) To be raised up (resurrected) by God on the third day. Ethics/morality, doing miracles, teaching in parables, and connecting with disaffected people were, at best, His secondary and tertiary concerns. If the heart of the unsaved is not redeemed and realigned with the heavenly Father, his or her every attempt at morality will prove futile. If miracles excite and amaze, there is infinitely more to the human struggle for meaning. If teaching brings enthusiasm in the continuing quest for wisdom, most will miss the ultimate purpose of Christ. Indeed, daily, we view human, secular, vain, empty attempts to reach God, aside from coming through His Son.

I have noticed that when prominent unsaved people (intellectuals, celebrities, authors, pundits, etc.) take to the public airwaves (television, radio, Internet blogs), aiming to explain their perception of Christian virtue, they stop at the catchall, *"God is love,"* or some other sentimentality. Interestingly, they extol

Christ as moral teacher, with the Sermon on the Mount as their chief text. They particularly affirm the parts relative to, *"Love thy neighbor,"* or *"Do unto others as you would have them do unto you."* Listening to them, however, I have yet to hear a reasonable interpretation of the necessity of being *"born again"* (John 3:3-7). Truly, any purporting to quote the Scripture, let alone fully interpret and understand it, first needs a relationship with God the Father, God the Son and God the Holy Spirit.

Like veneration of Dr. Martin Luther King Jr. by persons who, while he lived, were unsympathetic to black aspirations for freedom, equality and dignity, many "pick and choose" the emphases of Christ's ministry.

WHAT THEN, IS CHRIST'S AGENDA?

Please note: every productive, successful, beneficial meeting needs a clear, concise, compelling agenda. This truth references meetings of all kinds: corporate, political, academic, non-profits, congregations, denominations, clubs, or groups.

The defining objective of this chapter serves to remind us of the intentional perspective of our Savior, Jesus Christ; to plumb His overarching agenda. Once we have discovered that agenda, it stands to reason that His Church—faithful, obedient, ever-loyal, true—would emulate that very same agenda, in seeking to reach the unsaved.

Christians, or influential voices in American culture, in my view, really do not help themselves by imagining, guessing, or surmising what Christ's agenda entails, for He has simply and succinctly laid bare in every self-expression in the New Testament, in fulfillment of multiple allusions and prophecies from the Old Testament.

In the parlance of the day, let me cut to the chase: the utter, absolute, defining, non-negotiable, unyielding agenda of Christ involves rescuing and reconciling the lost to the heavenly Father, to advance God's kingdom.

1) Christ's agenda is clear: reaching the lost.

Through a preponderance of biblical utterances, Christ makes it clear that His paramount mission, His ultimate agenda, involves spiritual liberation of humanity from the incarceration of nagging proclivities (sin), the chief one being alienation from the Creator of the universe. Hear Him clearly: *"It is not those who are healthy who need a physician, but those who are sick...I did not come to call the righteous, but sinners"* (Matthew 9:12-13). Or, *"Come to Me, all who are weary and heavy-laden, and I will give you rest"* (Matthew 11:28). Or, *"I was sent only to the lost sheep of the house of Israel"* (Matthew 15:24). Consequently, Christ viewed His work as greater than teaching parables or physical healing. Indeed, He went to the very heart of what ails humanity: sinful separation from God!

If one remains unconvinced of the Savior's preeminent concern for the lost, the lonely, the languishing and those loitering in spiritual darkness, Christ plainly declared His supernatural, redemptive mission: *"For the Son of Man has come to save that which was lost"* (Matthew 18:11). It then stands to reason: what our Savior and Lord called His overriding mission must likewise engulf the interests of those who affirm their spiritual allegiance with Him (Christians). Let it be plainly stated: obedient Christians will introduce the lost to the Savior, so that He will save them. It is that simple and, for many, that complex.

Throughout this chapter, I shall reference those without saving faith in Jesus Christ as "lost," "unsaved" and as "sinners." These words are intentional, in that Christ in the Word of God makes the same references. I am mindful that, in our twenty-first-century world, many consider themselves enlightened, sophisticated, progressive, operating from post-modern analysis. Thus, such earlier bold terms might strike some as offensive. Without aiming to offend, I must be true to my Savior. He didn't go to the Cross, didn't suffer abuse, didn't hang there three hours for "happy," clean," "nice," or "kind" folks. Rather, He died for wretched sinners (including me, Hallelujah!).

Over two thousand years, two groups have been the special focus of God's love and grace: 1) those hordes ensnared in sin (the lost); and, 2) equal hordes willing to repent of sin, asking Christ to save them (the saved). Many of us rejoice in constituting the latter group, forgetting that God still yearns to reach the former one. And He expects to reach the lost "them" through the saved "us." Christian evangelism deliberately aims to reach sinners with the message of God's compassionate concern in Christ.

As improbable as it may sound, I am convinced that Christians hold the key to reversing negative trends of our present-day world. The open question remains: Are we willing to do the things necessary to make a qualitative difference in the lives of those still mired in life's entanglements? If saints will ever truly converse with them, sinners do want relief; they simply don't know how to appropriate that relief. Unsaved people know within themselves that life includes much more than the usual: a job, a large home, a new vehicle, going on vacation, purchasing appliances, home furnishings, a new wardrobe, school for their children, and taking in the news. Yet, such becomes the agenda of those seeking fulfillment, but trapped in the mundane. So, people trudge on, working, planning, dreaming and talking, incessantly, of better days ahead. Not much change occurs, however, because while change starts from within (internal disquiet), it must manifest itself from without (believing and doing something verifiably different).

So, I envision a fundamental change in spiritual condition, from lost (in sin), to found (in Christ). That's the kind of glorious transformation by Christ which fashions one into a *"new creature," as the old things pass away, and behold, new things come"* (2 Corinthians 5:17). Such newness far exceeds changing hair color, style, or length. It exceeds fad diets, liposuction, or colonic cleansing. It exceeds new addresses, larger domiciles or a better neighborhood. It exceeds enhanced job title, salary or benefits packages. It exceeds the new man, woman, or partner in one's life. Indeed, from the human perspective, what I am aiming for is an inversion of the value system. Thus, one views life from a decidedly new angle. Where, in the past, everything centered in what one could *do* for the betterment of self, the new perspective rejoices in what God has already *done* in sending His Son, Jesus Christ, to radically alter the trajectory of one's being.

2) Christ's agenda lifts humanity to unimaginable heights.

Christ's agenda, then, relishes the opportunity to lift humanity from its defeat, its despair, its doubt, its depression. Instead, Christ reverses the curse of sin, showing individuals their infinite potential in collaboration with Him. Thus, while Christ meets a person in his or her fallen condition (prostitute, drug abuser, alcoholic, liar, thief, adulterer, fornicator, pornography-addicted, tax-swindler, smug suburbanite, college student, bored housewife, successful businessman, promiscuous young adult, gay lover, whoever), He never leaves that person there. Spiritual transformation in Christ produces not a changed *exterior*, but a thoroughly new and different *interior*. My vehicle looks the same; but, due to its new engine, it drives so much better!

Saints of God praise Christ because He infuses life with meaning, with joy, with purpose, with direction. Incredibly, reflecting back on his life prior to embracing Christ as Savior, the apostle Paul infamously remarked: *"It is a trustworthy statement, deserving full acceptance, that Christ Jesus came into the world to save sinners, among whom I am foremost of all. And yet for this reason I found mercy, in order that in me as the foremost, Jesus Christ might demonstrate His perfect patience, as an example for those who would believe in Him for eternal life"* (1 Timothy 1:15-16).

While many might dispute the apostle Paul's self-characterization as "foremost" among sinners throughout human history, the point is well-established. He sought to acknowledge humble recognition of the extent to which God went in wooing and winning the former persecutor of the Christian faith. To His praise, God made a "trophy" of Paul, as He does everyone saved by the blood of Christ. Indeed, when sinners conclude, *"If God could save him or her, then, I know there is hope for me,"* God is infinitely glorified. Let that message ring out: Christ saves!

In the contemporary Christian experience, imagine God emptying the sainted choir loft, refreshing it with new converts to the Christian life, singing a "new song." Imagine an exalted pulpit full of recently forgiven, cleansed, baptized, called, anointed, sent men (or women), surrendered to God, anticipating even more conversions. Imagine, still, a sanctuary full of people new to Christ, worshipping with abandon, hanging on every utterance, greatly rejoicing in their salvation. When that happens, with the name of Christ, centralized, more will come down the aisles of a congregation, a Christian conference, or a Bible college. And, how refreshingly edifying that would be for the body of Christ!

If we embrace Christ's agenda, intentionally seeking the lost among us, we really won't have to stretch our imaginations. By obedience to the Great Commission, seeking the lost, wonderful benefits will accrue to the body of Christ. At certain points, I have exhorted our church fellowship with these words: *"Even if every existing church in our city were full to capacity on any Sunday, there would still be more people unsaved and un-churched out of worship."* Despite record numbers filling church sanctuaries across America, hearing stellar music, listening to prolific preaching, there remains more to achieve for God. Indeed, today, as we bask in best-selling Christian authors, large national Christian gatherings, celebrity conversions, glitzy publications, Internet presence, and more—there is still room in God's kingdom for millions of converts.

The Christian church must never rest on its laurels, confident that we are pleasing God because of what we term "success," if the net gain for the kingdom is still negligible. When rape, murder, and drug incarceration rates plummet, I will attribute some of that to a surge in baptisms. When families are strengthened, in urban areas, with men accepting their leadership positions, I will celebrate the Christian "revival" that some believe is already engulfing the land. When moral values are more prominently championed in the public square, I will be convinced that the Christian church is well on its way in lifting up the name of the Savior.

Yet, while Christians congratulate themselves on representing the Savior, we really need to prayerfully inquire of God: *"Are we taking Your love to the furthest reaches of humanity, as You commanded?" "Are we serving as agents of spiritual reconciliation, as You exhorted?" "Are we lifting the name of the Savior, as You made clear?"* Often, the Christian church feels satisfied in its mission, while the ultimate judge will be the Master. In analogy, many teachers feel they have taught; the student, however, must express if he or she has learned.

3) **Christ's agenda expects to engage Christians in pursuit of the unsaved.**

Christ's agenda, moreover, pivots on the Christian family actively "Going" toward sinners, rather than waiting for the lost to "Come" toward us. This expectation only coincides with Scripture: the Bible reveals that Christ leads sinners from the domain of "darkness" to the wonderful realm of "light." Note the Scriptures: *"...proclaim the excellencies of Him who has called you out of darkness into His marvelous light"* (1 Peter 2:9). Or, *"...to open their eyes so that they may turn from darkness to light, from the dominion of Satan to God, in order that they may receive forgiveness of sins and an inheritance among those who have been sanctified by faith in Me (Christ)"* (Acts 26:18).

Indeed, this "darkness" to "light" transition through Christ courses through New Testament Scripture: *"...for you were* formerly darkness, but now are light in the Lord; walk as children of light" (Ephesians 5:8). Or, "For He delivered us from the domain of darkness, and transferred us to the kingdom of His beloved Son, in whom we have redemption, the forgiveness of sins" (Colossians 1:13-14). Invincible over the enemy, Christ must pull the lost from their negative environments! The fact that He does so—for millions of unsaved—must be more widely shared with the lost among us.

It is, therefore, unconscionable for saints of God to leave the lost in the dark, groping for relief. Especially is their darkened condition troublesome, in view of the fact that we possess the "light" of Christ. Indeed, we hear the sobering injunction: "Let your light shine before men in such a way that they may see your good works, and glorify your Father who is in heaven" (Matthew 5:16).

When saints today rue the darkness—corruption, adultery, rape, insensitivity, murder, alternate lifestyles, broken families, theft, violence, abuse, despair, New Age religions, systemic racism, hostility and bitterness—they seem to forget their role: representation of the Savior in the earth realm. The Word reveals saints' binding task: "Occupy till I come" (Luke 19:13, KJV). By some unknown means, some have imprinted on the Christian church an erroneous metaphor: Christians are not defending a citadel, but rather acting as a conquering army. We don't exist to preserve territory; instead, we take more (new souls for Christ).

4) Christ's agenda is proactive in reaching the unsaved.

Furthermore, Christ's agenda is proactive, laser-focused, knowing that sinners exist throughout the world: on rural farms, in urban settings, on college campuses, on job sites, within families, in the mall, at the barbershop, at the beauty parlor, at the country club, within the fraternity, within the sorority, at the Rotary Club, on Wall Street, in the halls of Congress, at City Hall, at the White House, in corporate suites, in the unemployment line, at the service station, at the post office, at the pool hall, among the Boy Scouts, among the Girl Scouts, and every other group.

I appeal to Christians: slow down, amid all the hurly-burly of life. Take the time to really see the deplorable condition of those lost in sin. Again, it must be admitted, lost people come in various shapes and sizes: nice, loyal, kind people, home owners, friendly, tax-payers, those generous to a fault. Many believe they live happy lives. Their "lost" condition does not stem from evil intentions, bad behavior, or corrupt character, but rather, they have yet to embrace God's only means for a relationship with Himself: the Son of God, the Lord Jesus Christ.

In every expression, the Gospel of Christ represents Christ's agenda, conveying "Good News." This Good News transcends American citizens; in fact, it is global in its implications. So, it must appeal to more than the consumer capitalism of our country. The true Gospel is available to every tongue, every tribe, every color, every ethnicity, every culture, every situation, and every orientation. There is a wide socio-economic dimension to the message of Christ. That message includes all, and excludes none. Indeed, everyone can be a recipient of divine grace!

This wide net causes me to consider: in the New Testament Gospel narratives, we note Christ reaching out to all humanity, with an uncanny ability to relate to various despised groups and questionable individuals. That the religious bigots of His day (scribes, Pharisees, Sadducees) could not and would not accept His love for all is actually quite understandable, for they were elitists. Yet, He would not allow their elitism to dissuade Him from the central mission of His coming: to seek and to save the hordes of the lost.

5) Christ's agenda is unmistakably illustrated in His earthly ministry.

Note that Christ targeted sinners, which was clearly demonstrated in His fulsome conversation with a controversial woman in the Gospel of John, Chapter 4. There, Christ eviscerated every known barrier (racial, gender, class, religious, cultural, geographic, etc.) preventing full acceptance of one in respect to another. Significantly, by the end of their dialogue, the woman had been transfixed by divine grace: *"So the woman left her water-pot, and went into the city, and said to the men, 'Come, see a man who told me all the things that I have done; is this not the Christ?'"* (John 4:28-29). Her question at the end signified her full recognition of a gracious, non-judgmental, transformative, life-altering, redemptive encounter with the Savior.

Let us consider a critical reflection point and practical application. Today, in Christian circles, I pose some unsettling questions: *Do saints of God declare sufficient evidence of God's power to meet and minister to personal emptiness? Are repugnant, rebellious, repellant sinners welcome in our midst? Can Christ help those continually making serious judgment errors? Are baffled, bewildered, broken women coming to Christ? Are spiritually blind, confused men coming to Christ?*

Are profane people giving their lives to the Savior? Are addicted people celebrating their sobriety through Christ? If Christ is not achieving such powerful displays, the fault lies not in Him, but in our failure to bring the medicine (Christ) to the afflicted. A pharmacy is only useful to the degree that patients utilize its product. On the shelf, medicine is *potentially beneficial*. Once swallowed, it is *presently beneficial*.

6) Christ's agenda confronts the unsaved with "Good News."

Furthermore, Christ's agenda takes sinners into the vortex of sublime truth, the essentials comprising that to which Christ Himself committed, affecting the plan of salvation. The apostle Paul took up this "Gospel" refrain: *"For I delivered to you as of first importance what I also received, that Christ died for our sins according to the Scriptures, and that He was buried, and that He was raised on third day according to the Scriptures, and that He appeared to Cephas, then to the twelve..."* (1 Corinthians 15:3-5).

Quick question: Is the bulk of contemporary Christian preaching steeped in such Christ-centered, Calvary-based, blood-soaked proclamation? If not, we must recalibrate it, as the message of the kingdom of God will only find resonance in sinful hearts when such compelling, profound, transcendent truth is proclaimed in their hearing.

Finally, Christ's agenda accepts the limitations of people, while never leaving them in a vulnerable, broken, debilitated state. If we examine the biblical record, we discover that Christ worked to cut the cords of problem-plagued pasts, ushering persons into their present, previewing their faith-filled futures. People who came in contact with Christ started out blind, deaf, crippled, weak, bleeding, broken, bruised, sad, despairing, suffering and shameful. In most cases, after meeting Him, and then exercising faith in Him, the reverse became true: now, they were relieved, healed, set free, straightened up, able to see, with tongues loosened, walking in victory, with better, enhanced self-images. All of the change was directly attributable to coming to Him. What Christ did then, I can assure all, He gloriously does right now—on the basis of repentance, faith and full trust in Him.

For our purposes, therefore, Christ's agenda radically changes persons, from sinners to saints; from woefully lost to wonderfully loved; from once forlorn to now, focused; from depressed to delightful; from pessimism to optimism; from hell-bound to heaven-directed; and from pronounced guilty to acquitted in grace. While musing on this spiritual transformation, the Spirit of God reminded me of an old, yet meaningful song: *"Jesus Is the Best Thing that Ever Happened to Me."* Consider its poignant, potent lyrics:

"I've had my share of life's ups and downs,
God's been good to me, and the downs have been few,
I would guess you can say, God has blessed me,
But there's never been a time in my life, He didn't bring me through.

If anyone should ever write, my life story,
For whatever reason there might be,
You'd be there, between each line of pain and glory.

Jesus is the best thing that ever happened...
Jesus is the best thing that ever happened...
Jesus is the best thing that ever happened...

One day, I was lost but Jesus found me.

Jesus is the best thing that ever happened...
Jesus is the best thing that ever happened...
Jesus is the best thing that ever happened to me.

I was on my way to hell, but Jesus lifted me.

Jesus is the best thing that ever happened to me."

When more of the Christian family really believes and adopts that song's sense of the powerful, penetrating presence of Jesus the Savior in a life, we will urgently embrace Christ's agenda of seeking the lost with unparalleled enthusiasm.

7) **Today, Christ's agenda confronts Christian leaders and the body of Christ.**

Ultimately, Christ's agenda mandates that current Christian leaders (pastors, preachers, ministers, theologians, denominational executives, others) and Christian congregants affirm the Word of God, as it references the glorious spiritual transaction which alters destiny for the unsaved: *"So then as through one transgression there resulted condemnation to all men, even so through one act of righteousness there resulted justification of life to all men"* (Romans 5:18).

So, with the knowledge of Christ's agenda (reaching the unsaved with a supreme message of grace, forgiveness, and new life through His sinless sacrifice for their sin), I want to implore the Christian faith community: by all means, we must take up the same cause for which the Savior came to earth two thousand years ago. Indeed, we are His "witnesses." This is an obligation that Christians dare not neglect, for the souls of humanity depend on our obedience to His mission.

CHAPTER 4

Are People Really Lost without Christ?

Through these chapters, I aim to frame advocacy for Christian evangelism in a way that makes sharing faith in Christ with the lost the normative function of all Christians. I must at the outset, however, state categorically: the lost yet live among us! In order to offer the gift of salvation to more people, we must define our targeted audience. Inevitably, then, this examination raises a number of questions:

1) *Who are the lost?*
2) *Do they consider themselves lost?*
3) *How does the Bible define them?*
4) *How does contemporary Christian evangelism align with biblical patterns?*
5) *Are enough Christian entities employing the best strategies for reaching the lost in the name of Christ?*

Today, many intelligent, articulate, successful, high-profile people might answer the question heading this chapter (*"Are people really lost without Christ?"*) in varying ways.

Immediately, some might pose a further inquiry: "What do you mean by "lost"? Others, knowing that the word *lost* connotes "the fallen, depraved condition, manifested in the lack of a relationship with God," might profess to know God, even as they give little space to Jesus Christ, or "organized religion." Instead, they talk of personal "spirituality," even as they are unable to define or describe it.

Still others, grappling with an answer, might be bold enough to deny the very notion of being "lost." Instead, they may express their religious status: bold in atheism or agnosticism. From any point on the spectrum, people recoil from the notion of self-identifying as "lost."

Many feel as if that "lost" characterization smacks of severe judgment by others. So, quickly, some will express their mindsets as, "I aim to be a good person; I live by the standard of the golden rule: I treat others as I would want done toward me." Or, they quickly note that, "God is love."

So as to avoid the trap of circularity, endlessly going on about personal traits, let me state it clearly: America is replete with lost individuals. Let's consider the wide range of them.

1) Identifying Lost People

Lost people are quite often sensitive, compassionate, kind, erudite, charismatic, fun-loving, guileless, and charitable. Lost people are quite often cute, handsome, healthy, interesting, witty, creative, wise, patient, noble, strong, and loyal. Lost people are quite often caring, persuasive, decisive, attractive, innovative, reliable, dependable, and honest.

Lost people are quite often punctual, polite, professional, personable, helpful, outgoing and faithful. Lost people are quite often intelligent, successful, articulate, suave, progressive, confident, and daring, having many positive qualities.

At the same time, in candor, other lost people are quite often ignorant, boorish, belligerent, catty, wicked, perverted, haughty, hypocritical, bitter, stubborn, prideful, and resentful. Lost people are quite often mean, cynical, shameful, guilt-ridden, depressed, and objectionable. Lost people are quite often moody, tough, profane, vile, evil, manipulative, favoring the illicit and the pornographic, aggressive, and immoral.

Lost people are quite often enamored of, and deeply devoted to, fleshly living: hedonism, drug abuse, alcohol, violent displays, preying on the silly, weak, and vulnerable. Lost people are quite often nihilistic, narcissistic, egotistical, anarchistic, and rebellious against societal norms, while giving in to vacuous pursuits.

Lost people are variously characterized as African American, Anglo, Latino, Asian, unemployed, corporate, blue-collar, 1 percent, welfare, middle-class, impoverished, straight, LGBT, Democrat, Republican, Independent, Tea Party, non-voting, urban, rural, gun-control advocates, gun-toting, pro-life, pro-choice, red state, and blue state folks. From Main Street to Wall Street to Silicon Valley to the Midwest to the Bible-Belt to the coasts to the mountains to the prairies, lost people can be found everywhere.

Indeed, the variation in races, ethnicities, gender, age, orientation, and socio-economic status, all validate an inescapable truth: lost people don't necessarily look lost, nor act lost. Finally, they don't see themselves as "lost." But, in fact, unless and until they accept Christ as Savior, the Bible tells us, they are lost!

In the main, when I speak of the "lost" condition of humanity—really, those with whom we connect as husbands, brothers, wives, sisters, nieces, nephews, aunts, uncles, co-workers, classmates, and friends—I mean those frightened by doubts; those befuddled by long-ago choices; those drowning in guilt, shame and uncertainty; those trapped in moral confusion; and those intimidated by spiritual yearnings for something better, yet unable to capture the illusive "it."

2) God takes the initiative in reaching the lost.

The hymn "Amazing Grace" represents the repentant sinner as one who declares, *"I once was lost, but now am found; was blind, but now I see."* Even in this day of uplifting "praise" music, I recommend Christian congregations "dust off" the old, beautiful, biblically based hymns for their spiritual sustenance. Within this fact, however, it was God's initiative in seeking the lost (Genesis 3:9).

At the same time, the hymn, "Love Lifted Me" invokes the plaintive cry of one languishing in alienation, emotionally distraught: *"I was sinking deep in sin, far from the peaceful shore, very deeply stained within, sinking to rise no more; but the Master of the sea heard my despairing cry, from the waters lifted me—now safe am I."* Again, even as current Christianity emphasizes the positive while avoiding the negative, we still need to understand the plight of the "lost," those without a relationship with God through Christ.

3) What it really means to be lost?

While the above lists describe the beliefs and behaviors, perspective and practices of the "lost," the deepest similarity ensues from the fact that both groups—those who act lost and those who don't—*are* "lost" for one reason: either stubbornly or ignorantly, they have not embraced God's only solution for humanity's alienation from Him. In short, people are not "lost" because they are necessarily "bad" people. Rather, all are "lost" because they continually reject God's only provision—His Son Jesus Christ—for reconciling humanity to Himself.

Yet, in making this statement I must add a significant caveat: The love, grace, and mercy of God are especially extended to the "lost": *"For God so loved the world that He gave His only begotten Son, that whoever believes in Him should not perish, but have eternal life."* (John 3:16). Or, *"For the Son of Man has come to seek and to save that which was lost."* (Luke 19:10). Or, *"For the Son of Man has come to save that which was lost."* (Matthew 18:11). Or, *"But God demonstrates His own love toward us, in that while we were yet sinners, Christ died for us"* (Romans 5:8).

The cumulative effect of Scripture, then, reveals a clear love by God for those whom the Bible refers to as *"lost," "sinners,"* or the *"unsaved."* Of course, the terminology is not the highest consideration. Indeed, the poet hinted at the truth: *"A rose by any other name still smells as sweet."* Conversely, alienation from God, absence from Christ, means, definitively, the threat of eternal separation from God. Christian evangelism is motivated by several factors: 1) the love of God; 2) the sacrifice of Christ; and, 3) the portentous eternal condition of lost humanity.

4) Prominent Secular, "Lost" Groups

Specifically, in the American atheists, we note a representative cohort of "lost" humanity, affirming their right to live in non-belief. Against those favoring a "higher power," this group holds that none exists. Committed to widely spreading their views, the group hosts forums, symposiums, and an annual convention, maintains an attractive website, relies on other technologies, lobbies political leaders, and prepares adherents to debate religion, all while seeking to explain their views to national and global audiences. In short, these persons are unashamedly "lost," according to their perspective.

Moreover, atheists frown upon affirmations referencing God, calling such beliefs delusional, irrational, and superstitious, with those professing faith in Christ as feeble-minded. Many celebrate the Bible as a good moral primer, without crediting its precepts to God, whom they deny. None would view the Bible, however, as the inerrant, infallible, authoritative repository of divine revelation, beneficial for saving faith and discipleship practice. Also, many acknowledge Jesus Christ as, at best, an influential moral philosopher, with an agenda in alignment with contemporary left-leaning advocacy groups.

Acclaimed atheists include the late writer Christopher Hitchens, comedian Bill Maher, scientist Richard Dawkins, archaeologist Richard Leakey, the late actress Katherine Hepburn, musician Mick Jagger, investor Warren Buffett, Facebook inventor Mark Zuckerberg, former NYC Mayor Michael Bloomberg, writer Barbara Ehrenreich, Noble laureates, philosophers, and notables in varied fields: academia, jurisprudence, medicine, journalism, athletics, entertainment, etc. These individuals bring a distinctive ideology to religious debates, with intense emotional investment in their outcomes. With outsized influence due to notoriety, popularity and riches, these prominent persons have the ability to convince millions of the validity of their non-belief in God, in moral absolutes, or in guiding spiritual principles.

A special note to the redeemed, the Christian family, the body of Christ: many of the above-named ideologues, ideologies and institutions are engaged in all-out assault on godly values, biblical tenets, theological foundations, spiritual principles, moral precepts, and that which has guided Christian living for centuries, extending all the way back to the time of Christ.

Some of these groups and persons have unleashed scathing appraisals of the Christian viewpoint. They accuse adherents of practicing bigotry, intolerance, and narrowness. Often, because of their cultural influence, academic credentials, intellectual heft, political affiliations and financial acumen, they intimidate and then diminish the Christian worldview as silly, un-scientific and lacking in empirical foundations.

As a result, American and global cultures are being radically swayed in the direction of less devotion to God. As His existence and influence are questioned and minimized, it returns us to the critical inquiry: *"Are people really lost?"*

Another large group—agnostics—loosely organized, occupy a "grey area," holding that they are uncertain of God's existence. They assert that evidence for His existence points away from it. Leading intellectuals among this group argue from the world's chaotic, arbitrary, and unpredictable condition, that, if God does exist, He should exert more control of events. So, often, they raise the objection to His existence in the form of the question, *"Where was God in all of this?"*

Theologians use the word, *theodicy*, to capture the sentiment of how a good God allows evil and suffering in the world. Generally, this unsettling question arises in the aftermath of unprecedented human suffering: the 9/11 attacks, when terrorists killed 3,000 innocents; tsunamis in various countries, with vast devastation; earthquakes bringing loss of life, property and security; famine on a large scale; the African slave trade; the Jewish Holocaust; children senselessly murdered; the menace, rise, and machinations of evil dictators; and more.

Yet, the question looming over this message analyzes specific groups, identifying themselves as unbelievers. It seeks, further, to define the "lost" state, from a decidedly biblical perspective. Therefore, let us prayerfully, carefully, and humbly examine the record of Scripture, as it pertains to this crucial topic. The larger matter becomes how best to take the Christian message to those who are lost. Christians should especially target the unsaved for evangelistic success.

5) The Christian Message in Evangelism: Targeting Youth

The tactical consideration of Christian evangelism involves reaching all, but especially a younger demographic (18-35), with the astounding news of God's grace in Christ. For younger persons, searching for meaning, substance, and purpose, this Christ-centered message will prove invaluable. Social theorists argue that such young people suffer from a lack of absolutes, with what many term a "post-modern" worldview. Accordingly, contemporary evangelism might be called "Evangelism 2.0."

This "2.0" refers to technological emphases, like the many game systems favored by the youthful cohort.

In that sense, the Christian faith community should embrace all available technology (You Tube, Facebook, Twitter, websites and more), in reaching out to all, in the name of the Savior. Admittedly, for many of us who came to maturity in the 1980s, some of this technology is quite foreign. However, the body of Christ must never be viewed, by outsiders, as out-of-step with its cultural proclivities, or, else Christianity will be dismissed as "grandparents' faith."

6) Christian Evangelism embraces technology.

Today, creative, innovative evangelistic thrusts must, of necessity, be led by fresh minds, humble servants of God, well-versed in technology and social media. I would advise Christian leaders: find those persons who marry technology and Scripture in a way that reflects the character of our Savior. Let such persons design, monitor, and expand the technological outreach of, say, a congregation, seminary, or denomination.

As an example, the Roman Catholic Church, beginning at the Vatican and extending to the smallest local parish, embraces the available technology to reach adherents and to stay relevant with a rapidly changing culture, nationally and globally. Indeed, for centuries the Catholic Church, a bastion of tradition, has now come to recognize the incredible potential of the twenty-first-century world.

A local Christian congregation today, then, without a Web site, without live streaming of its worship, without a Facebook page, without Twitter, and so much more, seriously undermines its intention of reaching this generation with the Christian gospel. As increasing numbers of young persons blithely operate in a technological world (i-pad, i-phone, i-pod, android tablets), we must continually grapple with its meaning for advancing the kingdom of God through intentional Christian evangelism.

As the young are reticent regarding formal, one-on-one conversations, Christians need to discover new ways to connect with those whose world revolves around the latest technological gadget, or application.

Let me illustrate this point. As I begin preaching each Sunday, or other days, I usually ask persons to stand with me, for the reading of the Scripture text, honoring God in the process. Because of who God is, and for the revelation of His Word, I believe our standing reflects one way of extolling His name. Admittedly, I am "old-school": I read from a Bible. Increasingly, however, I notice more congregants reading the biblical text, while holding their cell phones or tablets. (Facetiously, I wonder: Could Dr. Billy Graham have won millions of sinners to Christ, "with an i-pad in my hand?") Just a thought!

My central argument involves the need to meet people where they live (in cyberspace, in virtual reality, navigating social media), while understanding the infinite potential of technology, as it is directed toward evangelistic ends: taking the message of Christ to the masses, by the power of the Holy Spirit of God.

In light of the hordes of hurting, confused, lost people, it behooves the Christian faith community to present them with the grace of God, mediated through the Savior. We should meet them, in the manner of the Savior: *"Now all the tax-gatherers and the sinners were coming near Him to listen to Him. And both the Pharisees and the scribes began to grumble, saying, 'This man receives sinners and eats with them'"* (Luke 15:1-2).

7) **Christians must intentionally reach the lost, the unsaved, and the un-churched.**

The Luke 15 narrative, quite insightfully, places our Savior "at-home" among lost, alienated, confused, troubled, broken, shame-filled, guilt-ridden, corrupt, marginalized, nefarious masses. This fact in no way indicates His compromising truth, lowering standards for righteous behavior before the heavenly Father. Indeed, the very reason for Jesus' coming to the earth realm was the necessity of His bodily sacrifice for the sin of humanity.

The popularity of the Savior among sinners emanates not from compromising spiritual or biblical principles, but from His loving embrace of those caught in the bramble of poor life choices. Nothing in His teaching suggests the diminution of rigorous righteousness before God. In fact, the opposite is true: He alienates some because demands of the kingdom are so "difficult." Please note John 6:53ff as validation of this point.

Indeed, Christ understands the nature of sin as selfish entanglement in a morass of debilitating decisions, leading to greater estrangement from the heavenly Father. In nearly every encounter with humanity, the Savior connected with those with obvious physical, emotional, and psychological challenges: Mary Magdalene; the woman with the blood disorder; the woman at the well; blind Bartimaeus; the Syro-phonecian woman; the woman caught in adultery.

In some ways, the cast of characters surrounding Christ are from the fringe, the lowest rung of the socio-economic ladder: outcasts, misfits, and untouchables. Graciously, He seems to have taken special delight in "hanging out" with the unsaved.

In the best sense, these people gravitated to the Savior because they found Him sympathetic, insightful, compassionate, kind, and generous of spirit. Amid an aloof, mean, cynical, abrasive, judgmental, censorious world system, lost people have found acceptance, safety and security in the warm embrace of the Son of God.

Specific to Luke 15, Christ seemed to go "out of His way," to affirm the worth and personhood of those captured by previous poor choices and questionable alliances. In that day, "tax-gatherers" were especially hated, seen by the Jews as tools of the oppressive Roman power structure. Tax-gatherers, or tax collectors, made their way in a system designed to profit from the abject conditions under which the Jews were forced to live. *"Taxation without representation leads to tyranny"* epitomized their everyday existence.

What made the situation utterly unbearable for the Jews was the proclivity of many tax collectors to solicit and accept bribes from poor people. In a day without calculators or computers, the tax owed to the Romans was whatever the greedy collectors said it was. Failure to pay by the Jews could be viewed as grounds for a claim of treason. So, most paid the tax stipulated to the hated Romans, giving it to unscrupulous tax collectors. Yet, the Luke 15 text tells us that our Savior welcomed them to hear "life-giving" truth!

From these initial verses in Luke 15, some critical implications ensue:

☐ *Did Christ really know the unsavory characters of those with whom He ate?*

☐ *If He did, why would He invite them into fellowship?*

☐ *Could Christ actually understand the depth of animus a single tax-collector generated, simply by showing his face to a Jewish crowd?*

☐ *Again, presuming that He knew this reception would foster deep hostility from Jews, in general, and Pharisees, in particular, why did He continue this practice?*

☐ *Why would Christ, intentionally, antagonize Jews yearning for a modicum of respect from an un-just political system?*

I am persuaded by illumination from the Spirit of God that, in fact, Christ knew the very heart of those despised tax-collectors and assorted "sinners" in His midst. By embracing those on the fringes of acceptance by the religious elite (Pharisees), Christ set a template for all of His followers: people matter and they especially matter to God!

Therefore, to demonstrate God's unqualified, inexpressible, unfailing grace, mercy, and love to humanity, Christ deliberately associated with those shunned by society. Indeed, in the remainder of Luke 15, He directed important insights from three parables, all pertaining to "lost" items: a sheep; a coin; a son.

God's ultimate objective in reaching out to humanity in the name of Christ is quite clear: *"...there will be more joy in heaven over one sinner who repents than over ninety-nine righteous persons who need no repentance"* (Luke 15:7). People's lost condition demands that Christ (especially now through His church) take the initiative in sharing saving truth.

Probing the Luke 15 parable for interpretive insight, illustrative content, and practical application reveals that ninety-nine self-righteous people who keep all the rules, rituals, festivals, while congratulating themselves on living "holy lives," without connecting with the lost, seems to bring no joy to heaven! Conversely, one sinner confessing sin, owning Christ as Savior, and beginning an obedient Christian life sets off "party-time" in heaven!

Beyond debate, God is lovingly concerned about the lost, especially as they admit their hopeless condition and repent of it, coming totally toward Christ.

Within the nuances of each parable, we conclude that the naive, trusting lamb might have been lost due to wandering away from the flock; the coin might have simply rolled under household furniture, rendering it useless to the woman until found; but, this son was lost through willful rebellion, pride, self-will, and hubris against a loving father.

Most know of the parable of the prodigal son because it closely resembles the bulk of humanity, chafing under God's direction of our lives. Moreover, we all identify with the repentance of the son followed by the road home, culminating in reconciliation with a kind-hearted father. The late Dr. Manuel Scott Sr. used to say: *"No preacher should ever leave that boy lost, broken, sad, lonely, disconnected and forlorn in the "far-country." Everything pushes the preacher to bring the boy home."*

The joy of life is that God welcomes repentant sinners "home," from the far-country of anguish, shame, defeat and guilt. And, like the parable, in grace and love, He orders a robe, a ring, sandals and a fatted calf. Here is the crescendo for the spiritual transformation: *"...this son of mine was dead, and has come to life again; he was lost, and has been found. And they began to be merry"* (Luke 15:24).

8) Vital lessons for Christians in evangelizing the lost

As the body of Christ, Christians should reach out to the unsaved world with the same tenderness the Savior displayed. As He loves the lost without limits, so should we. As He demonstrated compassion toward the wayward, so should we. And, as He articulated the way to a better life for those adrift from moral moorings, we should do the same. As His *"ambassadors,"* (2 Corinthians 5:20) we must represent Him well.

If people are lost without Christ (and they are!), what are the best strategies for reaching them?

A) Transparency by the saved

First, transparency on the part of the redeemed church of Jesus Christ reveals that prior to confessing Jesus Christ as Savior, all were in a condition the Bible refers to as "lost." Specifically, more saints of God must remember their past lives, before they were "found" by Christ. In honesty, every saint has a "before Christ" period: it might have been full of ignorant acts, rash behavior, illicit conduct, sinful associations, immaturity, profanity, promiscuity, and more.

In other cases, while many were nice, kind, and considerate, persons were also self-centered, feeling that God was remote, and aloof from everyday concerns. It is important that saints mentally revisit their past (going to nightclubs, alcohol-fueled activities, wild promiscuity, vulgar profanity, etc.), because only then can they develop a psychic connection with those still laboring under the illusion of self-sufficiency. A hint: Christians should be a bit more accepting of those yet ensnared in the flagrant sins out of which God delivered us!

Interestingly, those who should celebrate Christ's forgiveness adopt an attitude of *"spiritual amnesia."* They choose to blank out their lives before coming to repentance and faith. Perhaps Peter, Paul, and countless others in the New Testament would have feigned moral clarity and ethical rectitude in living before Christ transformed them. Instead, the Bible records the totality of their lives—warts and all—indicators of pre- and post-Christ lives.

Within the bounds of propriety, omitting names, dates, specific occasions, or offering lurid details, to say nothing of possibly destroying the reputation of others, more saints need to share their struggles.

If one came to Christ from a gambling past, for example, that needs to be expressed.

If, on the other hand, one was an upstanding, well-liked "sinner," that, too should be shared.

If one was ensnared by shame and guilt, that testimony of Christ's intervention will, undoubtedly, bless others.

On the other hand, if one came to Christ early in life, that will help others make an early profession of faith.

No matter the case, that hoary hymn of the Christian church tells of the blood of Jesus: it reaches to the "highest mountain" as well as descending to the "lowest valley." Christ's blood, then, reaches all strata of humanity, every class, every ethnicity, every race, every gender, every orientation, and every condition.

B) New converts to Christ should return to their old haunts to retrieve others.

New converts to Christ must emerge from the muck Christ lifted them from, aiming, by God's grace, to bring others out who are still in there. For most an appeal to return to the "scene of the crime" may seem counter-intuitive: *"Why would I voluntarily return to that old way of thinking and living?"* My response: New converts to Christ know the multifaceted ways many may ill try to excuse and avoid dealing with their lost condition. As recent Christ-followers, they are especially equipped to see through the façade of completeness, perpetrated by those seeking evasion from the "real deal."

People new to faith, also, have little tolerance for those expressing misgivings regarding faith in Christ. They now live by the creed: "If Christ saved me, I know He can do the same for you."

On the other hand, some who aspire to follow Christ in reaching the lost wouldn't know where to find them, aside from among the homeless, the obviously drunk, or prostitutes. Yet, lost people (from above) are upstanding, family-oriented, capable, prosperous, sophisticated, employed, and successful. At the same time, the unsaved are the least, the left-out, the lonely, and the languishing.

C) There are always "many people" ready to embrace Christ.

When I am tempted to think that only a certain group of people may benefit from refreshing waters of cleansing by faith in Christ, I am reminded of the Word: *"...go on speaking, and do not be silent; for I am with you, and no man will arrack you in order to harm you, for I have many people in this city"* (Acts 18:9-10).

The "many people" reference alerts me to the innumerable hordes of unsaved, un-affiliated, confused, and adrift, simply waiting for an invitation to real life through the Savior. Further, "many people" must include, by the context of Acts 18:1-11, a range of people: wicked, working, willing, and worshipping. Until they affirm Christ, they reside in the "potential" people category.

Once, years ago a Christian colleague alerted me to the difficulty he and his congregation were having reaching and enrolling new people (attendance was plummeting, enthusiasm was waning, and programs were few, with diminished financial support for the church's mission efforts).

In that fifteen-minute conversation, I cannot recall him ever saying, in effect, *"On the basis of our shortage, we should evangelize our neighborhood, or ask members the spiritual state of their friends and relatives."* Instead, it was easier to comment on the tough times, without thinking of the millions of unsaved to be reached for Christ.

Perhaps I can polish this point further, adding that, amidst economic downturn, social upheaval, political stagnation, family dysfunction, or relational strife in any American community or city, the most resilient entity there remains the Church of the Lord Jesus Christ. Of course, this is due to the "organism" having the promise of Christ's forever support: *"Lo, I am with you always, even to the end of the age"* (Matthew 28:20b).

Practically speaking, then, no Christian fellowship should lack for new converts, if some in that congregation dare to evangelize in the name of Jesus Christ. Absent some bulletin that no one yet resides in that area, we can believe that God still has "many people" in any community or city.

And, since I know that God does not bless churches for their inherent holiness, or merit (as He does not with individuals), I encourage Christian leaders to pray for, plan for, and prepare for new souls for the kingdom of God. My colleague (described above) didn't want to work for new converts; maybe, in a misguided way, he expected God to just "send them." How naïve! How lazy! How descriptive of twenty-first century church life!

D) Christian leaders and congregants must regularly emphasize evangelism.

If the identified lost among us are to be reached for Christ, heralding the advance of God's kingdom, pastors and congregational leaders must teach, teach, and then teach more, the importance of individual personal soul-winning. In most cases, lack of converts results from lack of effort. If there are no visitors in Sunday worship, there will probably be few, if any, at the altar, confirming a decision for Christ. God works through prayer, planning, and proclamation.

The most pernicious, insidious, dangerous threat to the vitality of the Christian church is the sentiment that God will, somehow, lead new people to the kingdom, through little or no involvement by His saints. That unfortunate ethos, verging on presumption, threatens the Christian church today.

What astounds me regarding hard-line, long-time leaders (political, corporate, sports, religious, philanthropic, etc.) is the degree to which they hammer home their governing philosophy: by passionate, persistent, consistent, and insistent labors. Despite changes and challenges, such leaders remain resolute in their core values, while promulgating them to an ever-widening audience of listeners and would-be disciples. While they are teaching these principles, it seems as if few may be paying attention; yet, over time, it is amazing how such views have been inculcated in the ones who were part of the group.

Some theorize that great lessons are both "taught" and "caught." Spiritual leaders, operating in the Scripture, especially in Christian evangelism, can only do the former, while praying for results in the latter. In evangelism, people may not verbally assent to the teaching; they validate having "caught" the evangelistic impulse each time they bring others to Christ.

E) Intentions align with achievements.

Reaching the lost, further, means being *"intentional"* regarding the spiritual process of leading another to saving faith in Christ. If our objective is winning a soul to Christ, we must not be satisfied with anything less than a "Yes" to the claims of the Messiah.

Christians must not take lightly the privilege of speaking the life-giving truth of ultimate hope in Christ. We have an explosive message to share with the unsaved, and they have unmet needs which are only met through the Savior. Thus, we should share it, unashamedly.

Also, when there is a targeted evangelistic contact (for example, a visitor in morning worship), an appropriate group in the congregation must jealously monitor that prospect, and all current information regarding him/her. Please consider my reasoning: the visitor now knows something regarding the church's teaching, its biblical stance, its worship style, its ministries, its length of worship, its "vibe" and more. If Christ resides at the center of that fellowship, we should relentlessly pursue—but not hound—that visitor, until he or she decides to commit there, or go elsewhere.

Indeed, if our objective is obedience to Christ's command to evangelize, it means meeting people everywhere we go. In the process, we must obtain names, phone numbers, e-mail addresses, and all pertinent information, so that we may reach a person at a later time and date.

F) Evangelism consumes "waking moments."

Many saints of God frequent similar places as the lost (car washes, malls, barbershops, beauty parlors, sporting events, comedy clubs, post-offices, banks, libraries, art museums, political campaigns, labor-union meetings, bowling lanes, restaurants, airports, hotel conferences, business trips, vacation spots, cruise liners, picnics, skating rinks, shoe-shine stands, and more). Within all of those venues, it is impossible not to run into some lost people.

So, led by sensitive spiritual leaders, individual saints must seize every opportunity to reach the unsaved. When the idea ("It may be later than you think") is driven home to all in the Christian Church in regards to the unsaved, we will use every tool in the tool-kit to reach the lost.

A grand strategy for connecting with the unsaved is recognition that every opportunity represents a significant one. Like a ripened piece of fruit ready to fall off the tree, we can never know just where, emotionally, another may be at a given moment.

During times of stress, loss, or severe challenge, many yearn for emotional scaffolding and foundational answers. So, we should ask God's Holy Spirit to prompt us toward a ready, seeking, vulnerable, pliant lost person. Without manipulating their tough situation, we share the goodness of Christ, seen in His dying on their behalf. Indeed, because of His grace on Calvary, all can enjoy the benefits of life: *"The thief comes only to steal, and kill, and destroy; I came that they might have life, and have it abundantly"* (John 10:10).

9) Christians aim to "change the culture" of lost-ness.

Finally, if reaching the unsaved represents the true objective of a Christian leader, congregation, seminary, or denominational leader, it must be repeatedly articulated. The best means of "changing a culture" comes from hearing spiritual, biblical, theological, and pragmatic views that express a new paradigm.

For example, a pastor signals a new direction for a Christian congregation by affirming that direction from the pulpit, in print, signage, written materials, and general means of communication with the congregation and with the wider world. That leader would do well in mingling with like-minded leaders, while bringing such "influencers" to speak before the congregation. All of this agitation for Christian evangelism saturates the atmosphere with expectancy. The same holds true for the leader of a Bible college or seminary, as well as those leading Christian denominations.

In the preceding paragraph I used a conditional word, "If," because it is never certain that Christians really want to engage in the mission of Christ. Such work is tedious, composed of expressing a vision for change, teaching it, modeling it, and gauging its effectiveness. Earlier, I asserted that if reaching the lost with the saving message of Christ were an easy process, some astute Christian leader would have long ago patented it: "Five Easy Steps for Christian Evangelism." While that title may sound interesting and inviting, I can assure all: nothing is "easy" as we work to lead persons out of spiritual darkness.

So, I close with restatement of several dominant thoughts: 1) There are lost people among us; 2) We can identify the unsaved; 3) Saints of God are commanded to reach the unsaved with the message of Christ; 4) The task before the Christian faith community is tough; and, 5) By the power of God's Holy Spirit, Christians can see and celebrate spiritual transformation of the lost.

In the main, we need some specific "call-to-arms" for Christian evangelism.

This notion remains incomplete unless we answer the question of this message. So, yes, persons are lost until they make the discovery of God's plan for their reconciliation, hope and future.

That divine plan, bathed in love, nurtured in grace, and abounding in mercy, was set from the foundation of the world. It required the Son of God to voluntarily give His life (supreme sacrifice for all). While I clumsily explain it, the Scripture states it plainly: "...*God was in Christ, reconciling the world to Himself, not counting their trespasses against them, and He has given to us the word of reconciliation*" (2 Corinthians 5:19).

Salvation must always center in what God did in Christ. And, His best work—far above teaching, above healing the sick, above moral virtue, above all His mystical ways—was reserved for a hill called Calvary.

On Calvary, Christ paid our sin debt in full.

On Calvary, His precious blood cleansed our filth from sin.

On Calvary, His Father accepted the act of His Son.

On Calvary, through Christ, humanity received transcendent hope, sublime peace, and the promise of the future.

On Calvary, because of Christ, a repentant thief became the template for our salvation, promised "Paradise," with all that accompanied it.

Yes, Calvary starts and culminates the process of human redemption.

Despite advances, maturity, scholarship, technology, and contemporary emphases, I still declare that Christ died for our sins! And, God raised Him up!

My preaching, of necessity, affirms that something super--natural occurred "early Sunday morning!"

CHAPTER 5

Why Christian Evangelism Matters

In the early musings, moments and movements of the twenty-first century, amid cultural flux and historical shifts, I fervently pray for the recovery of Christian evangelism (sharing Christ with others as the sole means of salvation) as the dominant consideration of the church of the Lord Jesus Christ. Saints of God must pursue the advancement of the kingdom of God in yielded lives through the Master. Christ alone is humanity's only, true and lasting hope. This evangelistic objective must be prayed over, reflected upon, celebrated, and widely implemented by millions of Christian saints, nationally and globally. In short, I am unalterably wed to an orthodox Christian theme: Christian evangelism matters! We should by all means evaluate the contours of this notion of evangelism.

1) **The Word affirms evangelism as the dominant focus of Christianity.**

The deep conviction of the necessity of evangelism rests in the Word of God, representing a binding, non-negotiable, preeminent mandate for God's church. That mandate to evangelize occurs frequently in the New Testament (see Matthew 28:18-20; Acts 1:8; Matthew 4:19; Matthew 9:37-38; John 15:8). By any measure, Christian evangelism represents the highest calling of God's people in every epoch and every season. In short, unlike certain fruits and vegetables, telling others, one-on-one, about our Savior will never go "out of season." Every day, then, represents ample opportunity for sharing life-giving truths regarding the Savior. Today, saints must examine why the Christian church exists.

The church of Jesus Christ, in my view, exists not to celebrate personal salvation, health, holiness, prosperity, or social-justice alone, but to extend the kingdom "franchise" to the widest possible circle of humanity (lost, wayward, immoral, un-churched, problem-plagued, sad, lonely, rejected, and forlorn people). Despite moments of confusion, caused by departure from our core mission ("making disciples"), Christians exist for a supernatural reason.

Let us note that every entity on Earth recognizes its essential reason for existence. General Motors (GM) Corporation exists to engineer and build, market, and service automobiles for the general public. Thousands of McDonald's franchises exist to sell fast-food to hungry customers. Apple exists to develop new technological products for a ravenous, gadget-centered world. Universities exist to teach, train and prepare students for professional achievement. Courts exist to adjudicate complex legal matters. Hospitals exist to help sick patients get well. When it relates to the church of Jesus Christ, however, may I raise an impertinent inquiry: *What forms the central objective of the Christian church?*

2) Varying priorities for Christians today

For increasing numbers, God's church (through leaders, congregations, seminaries, denominations, institutions, conferences, literature, emphases, and works) exists to facilitate worship of God, prayer, Bible study, living a sanctified life, or what some would term "religious ends." While many refer to *religion*, I choose to emphasize *relationship.* In the former, I try to please a holy God; in the latter, that holy God reaches out to me, through His Son, Jesus Christ. In the former, I call attention to *what I do*; while, in the latter, everything centers in what *Christ has already done.*

Other thought-leaders locate the objective of the Christian church in its moral teaching, forming the basis for ethical behavior, fueling societal enhancement. Still others assert that the fundamental "raison d'etre" of the Christian church lies in its advocacy for social justice in a world sorely in need of godly influence.

While I agree with these objectives, I am persuaded by the Word of God of an even higher, ultimate objective: *"making disciples"* for the kingdom of God. (Matthew 28:18-20). That sublime distinction must be widely articulated and greatly proclaimed. God's church has a unique mission, one greater than any other human entity.

In short, I contend that individual Christians, and the Christian Church, corporately, exist ultimately to advance the kingdom of God by intentionally bringing new persons to salvation through the atoning efficacy of the Lord Jesus Christ. Indeed, it is quite possible for the church to engage in many important works while failing to advance God's core objective.

3) Selfish Christians: sign of the times

Lately, the Spirit of God has revealed to me a dangerous spirit of selfishness among saints of God. Once they are saved, and learning principles of godliness, too many cease to have concern for lost persons all around them. Spiritual leaders only make the matter worse by failing to remind Christians of their mission in reaching the lost, beautifully articulated by Christ in the above Scriptures.

We attack the ills of current Christianity—lethargy, apathy, and ill-defined mission focus—when we recall our calling from Christ: *"making disciples."* If the above-referenced corporate behemoths (GM, McDonald's, or Apple), and other institutions forget their core mission, they cease to have relevance for the culture. Most often, people within the institution (Research and Development) are tasked with finding new ways to maintain connection to the needs and tastes of consumers. Perhaps the Christian Church needs some R&D specialists to keep it in tune with the needs of those (especially, the unsaved) in our culture.

On second thought: Christians already have such specialists— anointed pastors, godly congregational leaders, insightful theologians, and committed denominational executives. Through prayer, the Word, wide reading, reflection, working with other Christian groups and more, they can help shape the perspective of other Christian congregations.

Therefore, Christians searching for the lost, bringing the message of Christ, must assess their motivations, within the prism of a few critical considerations:

4) Christians must stay with the soul-winning mission.

When Christians fail to understand, articulate and pursue the central mission of Christianity, it imperils effectiveness for Christ. New converts to Christ add to and advance the kingdom of God. That is the Christian mission. That mission can only be achieved through directed tasks in the arena of personal soul-winning. There is, indisputably, a work for every saint in the sanctuary: hearing and heeding the summons to tell another of God's grace in Christ, ending the alienation from God. Sin separates, but Christ reconciles. That is the message we convey to the unsaved. It is one that is both simple and profound. It is one easy to express, but difficult to implement.

In the New Testament, the Day of Pentecost inaugurated a mighty move of God, as Christ the Savior was affirmed before several thousand hearers. Immediately following, some three thousand were saved (see Acts 2:41). Now, this large group grew in various ways: spiritually, relationally, and numerically. Daily, they were dedicated to teaching, fellowship, breaking of bread, prayer, sharing, and watching dynamic manifestations of God. Indeed, the name of God was honored. Like those pioneering saints, Christians today must embrace an expectation of new people coming to salvation and commitment: *"And the Lord was adding to their number day by day those who were being saved"* (Acts 2:47b).

If we obtain in life proportionate to what we expect, Christians must expect more from God! If we want new souls for His Kingdom, to glorify His name, to represent Christ in the earth, we must expect God to save, as we share His love in Christ. It's that simple and that complex. In another setting—Matthew 9—Christ makes it crystal clear: the harvest (pool of unsaved, un-churched) is always "plentiful." The only drawback involves a "worker" shortage. And the remedy entails prayer for more "workers" to bring in the harvest!

Our "take-away" concept: Christians must affirm their "main thing" (souls for the kingdom). And, they must keep that mission as the main thing! Throughout the Church Age, the Christian church has been engaged in a spiritual campaign, to take some away from the enemy's influence. Perennially, this evangelistic campaign has seen several peaks and valleys, ebbs and flows, starts and stops. In the campaign, critically, individual saints of God represent the tip of the spear in the quest to reach the unsaved with the glorious news of redemption through the Savior, Jesus Christ.

5) Mega-churches or "mega-ministry" emphases

While I am deeply respectful of mega-churches (2,000 congregants and above), with close colleagues serving such congregations throughout America, let me offer another definition of success in Christianity. It entails faithfulness to godly ideals: worship, Christ, biblical truth, prayer, Spirit-led, obedience, excellence, morality, integrity, holiness, creative ministries, evangelistic outreach, giving to Kingdom causes, community transformation, and more.

Objectively speaking, most American congregations (irrespective of ethnicity, locale, denomination, or social status) fall in the range of less than one hundred persons in Sunday attendance. That means everything addressed to the Christian church should appeal to leaders and members of small Christian fellowships. I heartily commend the work these fellowships are doing, to bring glory to God and advance His kingdom. Nevertheless, small congregations need to adopt a "mega-ministry" philosophy. Expect great exploits for the kingdom of God. Make no small plans for advancement when Christ is involved. Small yes; but, be effective in reaching the lost!

"Mega-churches," on the other hand, should serve as models of evangelism, teaching, ministries, community transformation and kingdom-orientation. When such large fellowships fail to represent the will of God, they resort to "maintenance ministry," with insularity the dominant theme (good, holy Christians obtaining insight, blessing, healing, deliverance, and prosperity). When the commitment to souls for Christ represents the dominant theme in congregational life, it leads to vibrant Christianity.

We need congregations to lead in dynamic soul-winning teaching. Reaching the unsaved must be taught and modeled. In the totality of Christian concerns, lost people must be our dominant thrust.

We highlight Christian evangelism as our priority, as the thing that matters most, because in its absence complacency sets in. Christian evangelism is critical because it recognizes the eternal dimension of the kingdom, while not neglecting godly responses to the challenges of today. In all its work, the Christian church, more than any else—over counting numbers—it makes discipleship its focus. The institutional Christian witness exists to foster quality, character-filled, prayerful, obedient, Word-oriented, Christ-exalting, Spirit-led, sensitive, loving, sharing disciples. Authentic Christianity, then, makes its presence felt, not simply in the sanctuary, at the time of Sunday worship, but, rather, in the streets wherever and whenever unsaved persons may be found.

In all things, the key to changing the narrative of congregational life—revitalizing and renewing—involves stimulating that group with new converts to Christ. New persons bring to the body of Christ questions, challenges, deferred dreams and more. Biblical revelation assists in evangelistic endeavors, in unusual ways, as we shall see.

6) A model for Christian evangelism: The Nehemiah Spirit

The Old Testament record of God's love for humanity reveals a simple, staggering, riveting picture of an unassuming, humble servant of God, Nehemiah. This man, surrounded by opportunity, privilege, and access to royalty, nonetheless, learned of the extreme privation of his people, the Jews. They were emerging from a prolonged period of divine retribution, the Babylonian Exile. In his exalted position, Nehemiah took initiative in rebuilding the burned, tattered walls of Jerusalem, to assuage their vulnerability. The task demonstrated unmatched skills in prayer, leadership, faithfulness, and organization. In the work he accomplished, Nehemiah embodied godliness, humility, integrity, patriotism, energy, creativity, piety, and unselfishness. Personal evangelism was immeasurably augmented, as some of those traits are used by soul-winners, operating in God's power, lifting up the Savior.

Current Christianity, aiming to reach new people for Christian discipleship, can derive valuable lessons from the Nehemiah model. Please note these principles from a dynamic man of God:

A. Prayerfulness—1:4ff

B. Strategic Vision—2:11ff

C. Hard, Smart Work—2:18ff

D. Defense against Assault—2:19-20

E. Creative Organization—4:15ff

F. Loyalty to Leadership—5:12-13

G. Extraordinary Success—6:15

Each principle, if properly instituted in a Christ-centered evangelistic outreach, will engender unusual success. The question is: *"Are we willing to work?"* In every endeavor, what separates achievers from failures is the degree to which some commit themselves to hard, ongoing work!

Indeed, songs are written, books penned, movies launched, inventions brought forth, technologies expanded, and movements begun, all because of work.

Evangelism, in essence, will work for Christian individuals, congregations, seminaries, and denominations, as long as they are willing to "work" at it. Indeed, there can be no success without some stress, in reaching out to the unsaved.

7) Christian work is Christ's expectation.

Rightly, godly, moral, ethical, right-standing people should not engage in profanity. For many, however, W-O-R-K resembles a four-letter word equated with something secular, bad, and vile. Too many run from it, strangely, while expecting spectacular results. Yet, nothing beneficial should come to one without a commitment to old-fashioned, sustained, stressful, hard work. This is equally true for Christians wishing to embrace Christ's evangelistic imperative.

Work, plain and simple, undergirds every successful venture, whether applying for employment, a home purchase, college admission, a rich relationship, or evangelistic outreach. As with all others, in seeking the lost, there must never be a quest for a "shortcut," gimmick, or quick fix, if we expect lasting achievement.

Christian evangelism involves going after the lost, seeing few results, yet still giving the effort our all. If "quitting is not an option" fuels secular achievement, even more so, we must exhibit dogged determination in Christian evangelism. Indeed, such engagement by dedicated saints of God seeks to change the negative trajectory of lives of the unsaved, which are devoid of commitment to God through Christ.

If the word *work* stymies Christian engagement with the lost around us (at the job site, on the college campus, in the neighborhood, among friends), perhaps we should replace it with "action." As intrepid followers of Christ, I am advocating bold, new initiatives in evangelism, ones designed to "move the needle," by way of seeing new converts to Christ.

Recently, I announced to our congregation my intention to serve the needs of long-term, resident members (preaching, teaching, sick visitations, counseling, etc.), while simultaneously seeking every possible means of reaching new converts (door-to-door campaigns, conferences, teaching, actively expanding the visitor pool). As a practical matter, I also expressed my heart-felt prayer that God would add three new persons to our fellowship per week.

Let me also add that, with a healthy fellowship (between 600-800 congregants), I am besieged with "pastoral" functions: sharing God's vision, preparing sermons, teaching Bible studies, visiting the sick, praying for various needs, encouraging the saints, counseling couples planning for marriage, presiding over memorials, processing mail, ensuring church bills are paid, raising the monthly budget, supervising building repairs, dealing with church staff, overseeing ministry meetings, and more.

Further, I have other *"ministerial"* functions: attending civic meetings, leading the prayer for community groups, sharing a vision for a neglected urban area, serving as the voice for low-income families, leading our radio outreach, writing well-received books, newspaper column perspectives, speaking across America, planning for a private "college preparatory" school for low-income children, and more.

If that were not enough, I humbly aim to give my all to "personal" functions: being a husband, father, brother, son, nephew, and son-in-law, with all that accompanies those varied roles. That means I attend dance recitals and school programs, help with homework, and celebrate graduations, and more.

To that list, persuaded that Christian evangelism really matters, I was now committing our congregation to aiming for three new souls added to the kingdom of God per week! That feat would require additional teaching and training. Indeed, some weeks, a dedicated pastor's work seems incredible.

Strangely, when I shared this evangelistic vision with some ministerial colleagues, it was met with a range of responses: "Man, that's great," "Yeah, I tried something like that." I even heard sobering quiet.

Honestly, what really concerns, confuses and confounds me is that energetic evangelism is *not* at the top of the priority list for many Christian leaders; accordingly, then, it is not a high priority for contemporary saints of God.

Against that view, Christ-followers should be the catalysts for evangelistic engagement. As optimists, despite what opinion polls in America reveal, Christians know that a relationship with God facilitated through Christ makes life worth living. Perhaps I am alone in this view; but too much negativity from media sources, along with pessimistic leaders, fuels the malaise of many regarding the role of government, unemployment, education, the general economy, immigration reform, blighted communities, income inequality, and the future. Where, I ask, are the optimists in our culture? Indeed, faith in God dictates that tomorrow will be better than today, and the prelude to a long life of fulfillment.

8) Christians need to capture the *Urgency* issue.

Christians engage in evangelism because of adherence to Christ's command, and we do so because of enthusiasm for people and their life-prospects. Also, we understand the *urgency* of the moment. Now is the time for salvation. Now we need to open our arms to the repentant. Now, more than any other time, we need enthusiasm for reaching the unsaved.

Specifically, when I reference *urgency*, I am reminded of an apt illustration. In the event of a fire, as we note persons in imminent peril, we extend ourselves for their safety. We scream to them, we call 9-1-1, we seek assistance from others, we use a water hose, among many helps. All that we do stems from the urgency of the situation. In the aftermath, especially as lives are saved, many will credit the swift, decisive, ongoing work of neighbors.

In a similar way, those of us redeemed by Christ are under obligation to "rescue the perishing," offering them a "lifeline" through our Savior. We know that the *"house"* of the unsaved is presently burning, viewing the flaming embers of poor choices, failed relationships, mislaid trust, despair, despondency, defeat, emotional bankruptcy, guilt, and shame. To them, saints of God announce, loudly if necessary: "Friend, you are in trouble; you need Christ in your life."

The Christian church, in my view, cares too much about being nice and accepted, in a defeated, decaying, and dying culture. *Urgency* regarding the lost condition of humanity without Christ should awaken us to our mission. I really do not want to mince words: Christian passivity, amid ruined lives, devoid of faith in Christ, really and deeply disturbs me.

Objectively, I hold, life is better when people possess an active, abiding faith relationship with God, made possible because of the sacrifice of the Lord Jesus Christ. Saved people, in my view, sincerely desire to exemplify Christ, seek more knowledge, grasp greater opportunities, and covet increased influence. They achieve these goals while transforming ideas, ideologies, and institutions sorely in need of reform.

Practically speaking, saved people should honor God, by working a job, marrying/producing children, voting in elections, maintaining health insurance, sending themselves and their children to colleges/universities, while expecting job promotions. Also, saved people should own homes, pay their bills in timely fashion, sustaining optimism, while representing God in Jesus Christ, in this untoward, ungodly world system. And, in trying times (debt, defeat, death) saved people have a built-in network of caring and loving support.

With all that our world needs, the number one need is simple: more godly people deployed with the expressed intention of leading others to the Savior, Jesus Christ. The apostle Paul makes the best case: *"I have become all things to all men, that I may by all means save some"* (1 Corinthians 9:22).

9) Christian Evangelism emphasizes Christ and "fishing."

Without apology, in the name of our Savior, I challenge pastors, ministers, Christian leaders, saints of God, the seminary community, and denominations, to "roll up" our sleeves, and plunge into the arduous work of *"fishing"* for souls (Matthew 4:19). If fishing in the natural sense requires travel, bait, a body of water, patience, engagement and more, the same will hold true in reaching and catching "fish" ensnared in sin, and still alienated from our gracious God. By continued secular, unsound, immoral reasoning, lost millions languish in disgrace, shame, and guilt.

Meanwhile, as experienced fishermen testify, sometimes they return from a fishing expedition without having caught anything. Most do not, however, allow that lack of success to dissuade them from trying again...and again...and again! Truly, determination to catch fish fuels every successful undertaking. Remember Peter's words to the Lord Jesus: *"Master, we worked hard all night and caught nothing, but at Your bidding I will let down the nets"* (Luke 5:5). Please catch (pun intended!) the overarching spiritual lesson: previous failure does not guarantee a present one. Rather, it prepares us for stupendous success, as Peter and his companions *"enclosed a great quantity of fish; and their nets began to break"* (Luke 5:6).

Today, in my view, among Christians, among the saved, among the born-again, within the body of Christ, it is time for "net-breaking" achievements in reaching and winning the lost to Christ! Because people matter to the Savior, they must matter to His saints. In short, Christian evangelism matters because unsaved people matter to God. They really do!

Permit me a word about a form of Christian evangelism: Even in our enlightened day, door-to-door, one-on-one, direct evangelism still yields results. The Jehovah's Witness, the Mormons and others (with the wrong message, but the right method) still employ volunteer sharers. What's missing for Christ-centered saints involves hunger for souls, the expectation that people will respond to the message. Yet, the Christ message is stunningly valid: *"And I, if I be lifted up from the earth, will draw all men to Myself"* (John 12:32). Despite years of practice, I'm not tired of uttering such "Jesus" truth. How, I must ask, about you?

Our prayers to God for wisdom in any undertaking, especially evangelism, should be supplemented by practical engagement. In other words, prayer and planning are critical for progress. So, once we arise from our knees, we must turn our heels toward those loitering in spiritual isolation. Despite previous attempts, many lost in sin are yet unable to change their spiritual condition. Too often, the unsaved pursue human-based "religion," whereas God offers Christ-centered "relationship" with Himself.

From diets to workouts, nose jobs to new wardrobes, plastic surgery to wigs/extensions, dentures to dental implants, people yearn for radical change in their physical appearance. Unfortunately, such emphases are external rather than internal ones. This means that the effort may prove facile, short-lived, and frustrating. Conversely, as Christ represents ultimate hope (and He does) in a world gone mad, it behooves Christians to present Him to the lost, the broken, the confused, the hurting. That's internal conversion, the best form of change. We boldly contend that humanity can only discover peace, joy and fulfillment through Christ. That's the non-negotiable Gospel message!

As the emphasis of this book (personal evangelism through Christ as humanity's only hope, both now and eternally) has deepened within me, I have come to view valiant attempts at improving lives without Christ as works in the Shakespearian formulation: *"full of sound and fury, signifying nothing."* Evaluate the contemporary quest:

Amass wealth; yet without Christ, it represents nothing!

Live in a mansion; yet without Christ, it means nothing!

Fly in a private jet; without Christ, it means nothing!

Relish a great education; yet without Christ, it amounts to nothing!

Invest in stocks, bonds, mutual funds; yet without Christ, it means nothing!

Enjoy a wonderful, warm relationship; yet without Christ, he/she is nothing!

Travel the world; yet without Christ, it profits nothing!

The Christian hymn, "Only What You Do for Christ Will Last" sums it all up. Note its sweeping lyrical content: *"You may build great cathedrals large or small, you can build skyscrapers grand and tall, you can conquer all the failures of the past, but only what you do for Christ will last. You may seek earthly power and fame, the world might be impressed by your great name, soon the glories of this life will all be past, but only what you do for Christ will last. Only what you do for Him will be counted at the end, only what you do for Christ will last."* That Word oriented message will yet resonate in unsaved hearts, if it is more-widely uttered by saints today.

10) Ending Christian inertia

The word *inertia* means "indisposition to action or motion." It also too often characterizes the contemporary body of Christ. Too often, saints of God are smug, satisfied, and stale. Blithely, we exist in the land of praise, worship, blessing, prosperity, and holiness, seemingly unconcerned with those outside, groping in spiritual darkness. Instead of *"Going,"* we expect the lost to, somehow, *"Come."*

Large swaths of the Christian witness go about business-as-usual, with a regular menu: up-tempo Sunday worships, national conferences, well-crafted seminars, best-selling books, national voices, assorted religious trappings. Too often, few lost are saved; few un-churched are drawn to spiritual fervor; and few are restored to faithfulness among the redeemed. It is as if the church were going about God's kingdom enterprise like an elaborate stage-play or motion picture: stage, set, actors, script, music, costumes, and action. Each Lord's Day, we play our "roles" in this drama, with little tangible spiritual transformation.

After the worship experience many Sundays, I am led to wonder: "Lord, were You pleased with our coming before You today?" Or, "Did we really come into Your presence?" Most often, I confess, I am afraid to await His answer!

Yet, in truth, I know what would please Him: *"There will be more joy in heaven over one sinner who repents than over ninety-nine righteous persons who need no repentance"* (Luke 15:7, 10). So, the ultimate measure of successful worship involves a sinner coming to repentance. By that measure, are Christians making inroads into the enemies' camp, bringing out the lost? Or, are we simply enjoying personal salvation, while focusing on the deficiencies of the saved?

CHAPTER 6

The Church Must Become Intentionally Evangelistic

A neglected area of Christian evangelism involves intentionally turning the local congregation "outward": motivate parishioners to engage with glaring community challenges, bringing a word of hope through Jesus Christ. As humanity grapples with a range of challenges, including rising debt, high unemployment, housing issues, income inequality, idle youth, climate change, human sexuality, political discord, family dysfunction, entrenched poverty, questionable police practices, blighted communities, health crises, drug/alcohol abuse, racism, poor life choices, and search for meaning, it behooves the Christian Church to present herself as a caring community in Christ.

"Outer-directed" Christian ministry, like a beautiful diamond, will include many brilliant "facets":

1) Christians must capture a Christ-centered "philosophy of ministry."

When the Christian church engages with hurting humanity, she faithfully follows her Lord: *"For I was hungry, and you gave*

Me something to eat; I was thirsty, and you gave Me drink; I was a stranger, and you invited me in; naked, and you clothed Me; I was sick, and you came to Me... And the King will answer and say to you, 'Truly I say to you, to the extent that you did it to one of these brothers of Mine, even the least of them, you did it to Me'" (Matthew 25:35-36, 40).

In simple terms, individual Christian congregations follow Christ as they engage with HIV/AIDS patients, advocate for better housing, champion healthcare, teach youth, care for the aged, contribute to community programs (the Salvation Army, Red Cross, Cancer Society, March of Dimes, Union Rescue Mission), advocate for academic scholarships, ensure food for the needy, assist domestic violence sufferers, reintegrate parolees, instill a work ethic, and more.

We never have to ask, "Is this the right thing to do?" In fact, from the New Testament narratives, we have the best answer to the inquiry, "What Would Jesus Do?" In His ministry, Christ spent considerable time with the "dregs" of society: those marginalized, outcast, lonely, sad, and forgotten. These "sinners" received Him gladly (Mark 12:37).

In several New Testament Gospel narratives, the cast to whom Christ committed compassion, time, and energy included women of questionable virtue (Mary Magdalene, the woman at well, the woman caught in adultery, the woman with alabaster box, and the Syrophoenician woman); twelve disciples from the lower socio-economic classes; lepers, swindlers, zealots, and others who didn't "fit" in proper society. In every case, Christ celebrated the inherent worth of individuals who possessed the "imago dei. " He was able to separate an invaluable person from one's poor life choices. What He did then, the Christian witness must aspire toward today.

2) Christians must change the dominant narrative.

Today, too many Christian congregations fail to embrace evangelistic zeal, in my judgment, because most are more comfortable with a "middle-class" model of valuable humanity. Those from stable families, with careers, owning homes, possessing education, exhibiting manners, wearing proper attire, having linguistic skills, and demonstrating good rearing are the targeted audience. They are coveted as new members of a particular fellowship. Yet, the world is composed of infinitely more dysfunctional people, who desperately need the love of God mediated through Jesus Christ. Until there is room in the congregation for "all" and "whosoever will," we are not faithfully following the example set by Christ.

When saints of God demonstrate tangible acts of love for the unsaved (broken people), it enhances attendance, fervor, and joy for that Christian fellowship. Indeed, the Gospel of Jesus Christ, soaked in His blood, is designed to reach both to the *"highest mountain"* and to the *"lowest valley."* In practical terms, this means that distinguished, sophisticated, well-groomed, well-mannered people need salvation through Christ in equal measure to those who are needy, lowly, broken, addicted, and homeless.

I challenge every Christian leader and congregation to make evangelism our daily prayer and dutiful priority. Every Lord's Day, every congregation should measure its effectiveness on the basis of seeing tangible evidence of new, transformed persons within its pews. The body of Christ exists to exhibit signs of life and vitality. What better way can we show this than new faces in the pews? A critical way of viewing God's kingdom work through Christ should also encompass support and engagement with community efforts.

So many agencies and programs working to alleviate human suffering need local congregational assistance: youth training, parolee-reintegration, cancer support, contributions to homeless shelters, partnering with domestic violence centers, engagement with schools, college assistance, tutorial outreaches, feeding the poor, offering youth safe places for recreation, and more.

3) Outer-directed congregations and saints serve Christ.

Moreover, outer-directed Christian congregations and saints will draw people, as those who are helped will reason: "That church cares about me Monday through Friday. Thus, I think I'll visit with them on Sunday."

Let us, then, rise to the occasion, to serve this present age, as Christian leaders and congregations known for prayerfulness, godliness, centered in the Word, exercising compassion, engagement, sensitivity, all the while Christ-affirming, progressive and dynamic for the twenty-first century world.

Most Christian congregations, if they exceed fifty years duration, have fought successfully against being a ministry concerned with only going to heaven, while too many around them live in perpetual hell. Indeed, a good charge for such a Christian group has always been the same: Let as many as possible experience the same joy, peace and hope in Jesus as we do. That commitment leads to community engagement in varied, non-traditional, cutting-edge, outside-the-box Christian ministries.

Medical professionals often ask patients a series of questions, based on observed vital signs: weight, blood pressure, stress level, headaches, nausea, balance, a smoker, or drinker? In some way, a Christian congregation should be evaluated by the divine Physician: are there new converts, ministries, or new emphases? Such "spiritual" signs indicate healthy or sick congregations. Accordingly, we repeat a central thesis of this book: new persons embracing the Christ ideal, as "babes in Christ," seeking tenets of Christian discipleship immeasurably strengthen a congregation.

With so many congregations of the "autonomous" variety (not under the control of a bishop, or central ecclesiological council), no one verifies vitality in that fellowship by some written, documented set of criteria (new members, baptisms, annual income, major projects, etc.) The result is leadership self-evaluation: if leaders say the church is making progress, all in the community accept that assessment. Nowhere else, I would submit, would an other entity judge itself. If so, corporate CEOS would not need fiduciary responsibility of a board of directors. If so, school superintendents wouldn't need administrators, teachers, and student evaluations. If so, athletic teams could go on losing, without firing the head coach. Yet, the Christian church persists, without evaluation.

4) The Christian Church illustrates principle and pragmatism.

Despite our desire to reach all humanity, especially those mentioned by Christ in Luke 4 (poor, downtrodden, blind, broken-hearted, etc.), we acknowledge that some do not regularly attend Christian worship for a variety of reasons. Let us assess these:

Common Reasons People Say They Don't Regularly Attend Worship:

    A. Worship holds too long.

    B. Worship conflicts with Sunday activities.

C. Churches are only concerned with money.

D. The sermons are boring and irrelevant to life.

E. The church is full of phony, hypocritical people.

F. Last time they came, church people were cold.

G. There are so many churches, still so many problems in society.

H. It's good for children, but not for adults.

I. They intend to stop certain practices before they come to God.

J. They don't understand church language, or the Bible readings.

K. They were forced to come as a child; now, they won't attend as an adult.

L. They have good intentions, but they forget each week.

M. They are tired from Saturday night activities.

N. For many men, it doesn't seem the "manly" thing to do.

O. Many haven't been invited by a dedicated saint of God.

In every case, we must understand the "excuses" people offer for failing to give their lives to Christ, as well as why they fail to regularly attend Christian worship. Take the above list as suggestive of the many reasons many among us fail to worship God.

5) Understanding twenty-first century culture helps Christian evangelism:

A. Lack of absolutes: amorality.

B. Faulty theory: "many roads" to salvation.

C. National malaise: Debt, lack, and shortage mentality.

D. Consumerism and "me" emphasis.

E. Loss of principle of sacrifice and service.

F. "Spirituality" without Christ!

G. "Spirituality" without the church.

H. Post-modernism.

I. Techno-centric, globalization.

J. Diversity, ethnicity, and pluralism.

K. Mass money-mania.

L. Loss of trust in leaders, institutions and high ideals.

M. No "big idea" or dominant social concern.

6) Christ furnishes the model for Christian engagement today.

The familiar Luke 4:18-19 passage captured Christ earnestly concerned with four audiences:

A. The poor

B. The captives

C. The blind

D. The downtrodden

While it may be tempting to make these persons "categories," rather than actual people, I submit that Christ literally reached out, with divine grace, to the poor (economically-challenged, destitute, broke, lower-class) people. Consider the people He targeted for miracles.

Second, Christ came to the earth realm, sent by God, to redeem those who are captives (to drugs, relationships, ways, attitudes, beliefs and behaviors). In many cases, such persons are incarcerated by the limitations of their own thinking. Through Christ, and His work on Calvary, however, there is spiritual liberation (John 8:36).

Third, we have ample evidence of Christ connecting with those who were both literally blind (Bartimeus, Mark 10:46; the man born blind, John 9; and the others), along with the spiritually blind (Saul, Acts 9). Either way, the need is for light (revelation) from God, eternally transforming meager existence. Arguably, in the twenty-first century, the most miserable are those whom *"the god of this world has blinded the minds of the unbelieving, that they may not see the light of the gospel of the glory of Christ, who is the image of God"* (2 Corinthians 4:4). Enmity and strife between and among races, also, stems from blindness: *"But the one who hates his brother is in the darkness and walks in the darkness, and does not know where he is going because the darkness has blinded his eyes"* (1 John 2:11). In short, sin blinds humanity!

Fourth, we note that Christ engaged with the "down-trodden" of His society, to such a degree that the Jewish religious establishment turned against Him. Despite religionists' taunts, Christ spent considerable time and energy pointing His grace toward paralytics, lepers, the marginalized, the maimed, the despised and others of that ilk. The contemporary challenge for the Christian church asks, "Who visits our worship each Sunday?" Are they solidly "middle-class," or are they from the ranks of the downtrodden? If we in Christendom connect with a class apart from those who caught the attention of Christ, what does that say about us?

An evangelistically-engaged leader, congregation, seminary, and denomination will ask itself deeply probing questions: *Are we making a difference in our community? Are unsaved persons responding to our appeal? Are we doing all we can, in the name of the Savior, to reach the lost in our midst? Is our message of hope in Christ sufficiently clear, that all may either accept or reject Christ as Savior?*

The larger Christian faith community (particularly seminary professors, leaders and Bible college personnel) assists local leaders and congregations by holding them accountable for adherence to the mission of Christ: reaching the lost. Of course, it really helps their case when such "constructive criticism" emanates from those aligned with the Christian church as faithful followers of Christ.

7) A hurting world needs a healing Christ.

Either a casual or concerted observation of contemporary times reveals that, for many, our day presents formidable challenges. Radio, television and Internet news bring human suffering and spiritual alienation to us via hand-held devices and other means. The Internet, particularly, draws us to often raw depictions of humanity's need for God and salvation through Christ as never before. YouTube entertains us, while Twitter reveals our need for self-expression. All depict symptoms of a hurting world.

Twenty-first-century life reveals a hurting world: corruption, murder, rape, abuse, violence, senseless murder, raw, perverted sexuality, political discord, Internet predators, "bullying," political scandal, new laws affirming "medicinal" drugs, rampant school dropouts, despair, loss of hope, nihilism, apathy, insensitivity and more. The by-word of our times has become, "whatever."

Moreover, professional sports no longer offer escape and entertainment, with players exhibiting poor judgment on and off the field, while crass, racist owners plague all leagues. In all sports, owners and players bicker over billions in revenue, while American unemployment still is too high. Consider the implications: middle-class fans subsidize a game owned by billionaires and played by millionaires! Even pointing out this idiocy only serves to highlight the extent of emotional hurt in our land. Entertainment (at astronomical costs!) serves as temporary relief from the pain of living. Even gossip concerning celebrity peccadilloes does not heighten individual lives.

Further, the hurt of humanity is reflected in many allowing depictions of the crass, negative, and toxic to flood their thoughts. Seemingly without end, family, friends, co-workers, and neighbors continue along a path of poor choices, dead-end relationships and numbing activities, all the while seeking something better. The vicious cycle can only be broken through divine intervention. Only Christ breaks the cycle of hurt and pain. Only Christ carries the answer for humanity's longing. Only Christ shows us the "more excellent way."

The more the daily news causes committed Christians to shake their heads in wonderment, the more we should understand the plight of the unsaved among us. And, the more our evangelistic impulse should be awakened. Christian evangelism should be the remedy for the ills visiting our land, like a scourge or a deadly plague. Despite the challenge, the answer is yet our Lord Jesus Christ. In Him, we discover "new life," and "new hope."

8) To view conversions, Christians must testify of God's grace in Christ.

To be effective in reaching the unsaved in a hurting world, more Christian saints must share knowledge of what Christ achieved in them. When saints share the extent to which Christ reached down in grace, lifting them to respectability, it dispels the notion of the Christian church being full of perfect people. There should be a sense of, "Well, if God in Christ saved him, I know there is hope for me." Thus, a personal testimony proves compelling, powerful and encouraging to the lost, the un-churched, and the unsure.

A report of a changed life through Christ becomes irrefutable for skeptical family, friends and neighbors. Recall the reaction of those who heard of God's work in the life of Saul, making him a disciple and promoter of the Christian cause he had previously sought to destroy: *"Lord, I have heard from many about this man, how much harm he did to Thy saints at Jerusalem; and here he has authority from the chief priests to bind all who call upon Thy name"* (Acts 9:13-14). What if God, similarly, has in mind a great evangelistic ministry, but He simply awaits you and me engaging with persons within our circle of contact? Who might that Saul/Paul be? Since we cannot know who it may be, we should approach every potential saint as key to kingdom expansion, in the name of our Savior, Jesus Christ.

Like Paul's testimony, a good testimony should have at least three elements:

A. Life before Christ;
B. How one met Christ; and,
C. Life since Christ.

Without shame, we need more Christians who are willing to share the details of their lives prior to confessing Christ as Savior. Sinners need to know that, truly, God saves, irrespective of a past, sin-stained, crooked life. In a callous world, sinners need to know there is hope for them.

9) Faithful Christians "earn the right" to share their faith in Christ.

A well-established, meaningful relationship fosters a conducive atmosphere for Christian evangelism. When people feel that someone truly cares about them, they tend to drop "defenses," opening new areas of themselves to others. This means that as one spends time talking and learning about another, then one may ask of their spiritual status. (In fact, through conversation and observation, you will learn what this friend appraises as valuable.) After sports, politics, current news, weather, gossip, employment, travel, and significant relationships, most people affirm the reality of what undergirds them. Listen carefully and non-judgmentally. As the Spirit of God leads, interject where you stand spiritually.

I've found that people will talk for hours, provided such talk references their favorite subject: them! Go ahead and indulge them. In so doing, we build a valuable bridge for future conversations about Christ.

When one has earned the right to share, tell of your favorite subject: the glorious change in you produced by the indwelling Savior, Christ. Give weight to your beliefs by describing your internal transformation. People expect you to tell of your "perfect" life. Stay true to what God has done for you in Jesus Christ. Put the emphasis on the new you!

Unsaved people must discern compassionate concern by the Christian faith community. Even as Christians stand for biblical ideals (heterosexual marriage, life beginning at conception, the immorality of fornication and adultery, living lives of integrity, and more), often directly contradicting secular-human desires, we can do it in love. I call this stance "principled pragmatism": affirm the Word, while celebrating God's grace in Christ.

In everyday living, principled pragmatism means that Christians understand the stresses, struggles, stumbles, situations, and, dare I say, strivings of the unsaved. Understanding another's worldview does not mean full agreement with it. Without Christ as Savior, the human predicament is dire and futile. That is why millions live in agony: no spiritual, biblical, or moral compass guides them. Rather, they live "flesh-dominated" existence. Christians, however, point unbelievers to the Savior.

10) In Christian evangelism endeavors, we must prioritize Scripture.

Often, today, evangelistic engagement success is scuttled by too great an emphasis on the pastor, preaching, congregation, worship duration, pristine edifice, facility amenities, church location, programs, ministries, the "fun" factor, and other insignificant considerations. Instead, everything in the supernatural realm rests on the foundation of Jesus Christ and His gracious deeds on the Cross, on behalf of sinners, those alienated from God.

In some Christian venues biblical preaching, developed from careful study of words of the biblical text and insightful interpretations that explore literature, language, genre, grammar, verb tense, voice, mood, context, environment, and more, excites, rather than strengthens, saints of God. Then, incredibly, some messages entirely miss the Savior! "Great" sermonizing fails, in my judgment, because its Christ-content proves lacking.

In other circles, the aim is "relevance," with the result being a saccharine, positive, watered-down version of the Gospel, making it little more than motivational gruel. Sometimes, in the haste to connect with this cynical culture, reference is made to an ill-defined "Him." Again, great sermonizing may come at the expense of the Christ message. As for me, I tell our congregation: "I must call the name of Jesus in every worship experience."

Moreover, we need more Christ messages (His birth, sinless sacrifice, suffering, death, entombment, and, the crescendo, God raised Him up, bodily!). I rest within the biblical standard: *"I am not ashamed of the gospel, for it is the power of God for salvation..."* (Romans 1:16). What we know regarding Christ, of necessity, comes to us by divine revelation.

Thus, Scripture offers the plan of salvation, infinitely better than the best, most eloquent spokesperson for the cause of Christ. Please recall that the Apostle Paul gives us the central message: *"Now I make known to you, brethren, the gospel which I preached to you, which also you received, in which also you stand, by which also you are saved, if you hold fast the word which I preached to you, unless you believed in vain. For I delivered to you as of first importance what I also received, that Christ died for our sins according to the Scriptures, and that He was buried and that He was raised on the third day according to the Scriptures, and that He appeared to Cephas, then to the twelve...and last of all, as it were to one untimely born, He appeared to me also. For I am the least of the apostles, who am not fit to be called an apostle, because I persecuted the church of God. But by the grace of God I am what I am, and His grace toward me did not prove vain; but I labored even more than all of them, yet not I, but the grace of God with me"* (1 Corinthians 15:1-10).

In that long passage of Scripture, Paul makes it abundantly clear that, contrary to our current fetish with "person-centered" religion, we have a "Christ-centered" relationship with our gracious God.

11) For Christians, we need to view privilege in sharing Christ.

Far from some onerous burden, more saints of God should rejoice in the wonderful privilege of sharing Christ as Savior with the unsaved. Think about it: God uses simple, frail, flawed, insignificant creatures—you and me—to tell of His grace, mercy, and love. When we consider it, God could have used other means.

God could have deputized birds to sing His grace, carrying that glorious message on their wings, to far-flung places. He could have employed animals to roam far and wide, bearing coded language of His peace. He could have allowed oceans and rivers to flood the message of fellowship with His human creation. He could have drafted the mighty oak, and the towering sequoia trees, to express His majesty, all conveying compassion for corrupt humanity. But, instead, He decided to use us! For that privilege, I give Him all the praise!

Yes, it is a privilege to declare, "Jesus saves." It is a privilege to proclaim His saving power. It is a privilege to tell all He has done for me. It is a privilege to lead another to sublime truth. It is a privilege to watch as the shackles of pride fall. It is a privilege to see guilt and shame obliterated, under the avalanche of cleansing by Christ's blood.

The fact of that glorious privilege given to transformed saints of God, made alive in Christ, must shape intentional evangelistic engagement by the Christian faith community. Let us reach the unsaved with boldness, courage, and love, knowing that both time and eternity will be shaped by Christian outreaches and reception by those faltering in sin. With time being short, saints must immediately rush to fulfill their evangelistic mission.

CHAPTER 7

Renewing Soul-winning Zeal

At the memorial of a beloved mentor, Dr. A. Louis Patterson of Houston, a distinguished Christian leader, it was revealed that, over 40 years of creative evangelistic engagement, he and his congregation were responsible for thirty-three thousand persons embracing the Christian Gospel. I highlight this fact because dedicated Christian leaders are quite influential in evangelistic successes. Indeed, the Bible challenges godly leaders to cultivate a culture of evangelistic engagement on the part of every individual in that fellowship of believers. Through sermons, teachings, printed materials, announcements, and personal modeling, pastors must recognize their God-ordained responsibility for developing passion within congregants for new souls for the kingdom of God.

The Christian fellowship (above) celebrating thirty-three thousand souls won to God's kingdom achieved this remarkable feat through a simple methodology: every Saturday morning, a group from the church ventured into its surrounding neighborhoods, armed with Bibles, tracts, and survey forms. In parks, at front doors, school sites, and on corners, they would engage "whosoever" in a critical conversation centering on the individual's spiritual standing before God. Many attempts at dialogue, we can be sure, resulted in negative comments, evasions and outright hostility. Nevertheless, this ministry, known as the SWAT Ministry ("Soul-Winners Action Team") continued. The pastor and members believed that they were glorifying God through proclaiming Christ as humanity's only Savior. I am motivated by their zeal for souls!

We need to emphasize a central truth: as pastors recognize the importance of Christian evangelism in the twenty-first century, it filters into the thinking of all alert congregants. We celebrate the work of God's Holy Spirit when He puts the "burden" for souls on the pastor's heart. Daily, weekly, monthly, yearly, the congregation begins to discern the supernatural dimension of the kingdom of God. The objective will be full deployment of the entire Christian fellowship in their respective spheres of influence, with a single message: Christ alone saves!

I cite this wonderful example of Bible-mandated, Christ-exalting, pastor-led, congregation-embraced Christian evangelism because many today wonder as to the efficacy of one-on-one sharing of the Christian faith. Indeed, it still surprises me that many Christian leaders, faced with dwindling Sunday attendance in worship, refuse to encourage parishioners to engage in the central mission of the Christian church: to present Christ in the power of the Holy Spirit to every unsaved person with whom we have any connection—family, friends, neighbors, and co-workers. Yet, from the Scripture, Christian evangelism stimulates God's Church, emotionally, spiritually, numerically, pragmatically, and financially. But, the highest rationale for Christian evangelism is the most sublime one: it was commanded by Christ, when He called His church to "make disciples" (Matthew 28:19).

Presented with proven results from evangelistic engagement with the wide range of humanity, I am persuaded to ask some penetrating questions of the body of Christ:

- [ ] What happened to Christian fervor for the lost—the unsaved?
- [ ] What happened to boldness in sharing Christ as ultimate Savior?
- [ ] What happened to full sanctuaries, with worshippers intent on reaching new people for Christ?
- [ ] What happened to deployed thousands, inviting the lost to enjoy the grace, mercy and love of God in Christ?
- [ ] What happened to enthusiasm by Christian saints, seasoning their conversations with the redeeming work of the Savior?
- [ ] What happened to dynamic congregations, infused with "fire" from the Holy Spirit, compelling saints to seek tangible results among the lost?

Clearly, Christ is still able to save; the Word of God remains inerrant, infallible, alive, authoritative, and relevant as spiritual revelation from God; the Holy Spirit still convicts of sin; sinners remain in our midst; heaven still rejoices over one who repents; and we yet have mouths with which to share Christ's message of liberation from the bondage of guilt, shame, and loneliness.

A serious hindrance to wide Christian mobilization for effective evangelism involves confusion between the words *organism* and *organization*. Though the words sound similar, there is a vast difference in them. If this confusion continues, it will negatively impact the present-day Christian movement in the world.

As an *organism*, by definition, the Christian movement is alive, vibrant and pulsating, just as is our Christ, whom we celebrate. Accordingly, as an organism, we dedicate ourselves to spiritual disciplines: worship, meditation, reflection, prayer, fasting, studying the Word, walking in obedience, calling on Jesus, living sanctified lives, exhibiting humility, exemplifying transformed character, relying upon the guidance of the Holy Spirit, giving to kingdom causes, sharing our faith in Christ, and changing societal norms, amid a myriad of godly traits.

At the same time, the Christian movement, of necessity, appreciates vital aspects of *organization*: leadership, constitution, by-laws, budgets, properties, machinery, methodology, sanctuaries, pews, lighting, sound systems, office staff, choirs, robes, uniforms, ushers, greeters, ministries, deacons, trustees, stewards, elders, protocol, and chain-of-command, again, among many important functions and functionaries.

In considering these two notions, I pray that Christian leaders, theologians, denominational leaders, and congregants will never forget the proper order: *organism* must dominate *organization*. Otherwise, Christians will engage in common maintenance rather than their central mission. If done properly, when Christians "go out," sinners will "come into" the glories of new life in Christ. That is what the kingdom of God through Christ ultimately champions in the world today.

Meeting Sundays for worship (people packing pews, grand edifices, lofty music, robed choirs, persuasive, eloquent preaching, and giving to various causes) all seems good; but, an element is missing: Where is the emphasis on the unsaved? Without it, saints of God become quarrelsome, fidgety, and confused.

If the mission of Christ ("making disciples") is not served, our gathering becomes trite, dull, stale and inert, no matter the size of the building, the budget, acclaim of the minister, or standing of the congregation. Authentic Christianity measures adherence to Christ's call in one way: souls saved for the kingdom of God!

For those today who, sanctimoniously, object to a fixation on numbers saved, or tracking numeric growth, I counter with the explosive growth of the early church in Acts 2:37-41. On the Day of Pentecost, with thousands in attendance, after the stellar, Christ-centered message from the reclaimed denier, Peter, God used that message to redeem some 3,000 in one day! The 3,000 *received his word, and were baptized*" (Acts 2:41). Now, somebody had to count the results! Moreover, later the numbers continued to rise, with God *"adding to their number day by day those who were being saved"* (Acts 2:47b).

Since the Adversary (the devil) has, over the centuries, won so many, it just seems to me that believers ought to win some. Clearly, the devil orchestrates heartache, suffering, shame, guilt, despair, alienation and bitterness. It is his job, to which he has committed himself, and, by any measure, one he has successfully undertaken. So, now, redeemed saints of God should celebrate positive territory —"winning some"—by inviting the lost to new life in Christ. When new converts to Christ are filled with forgiveness, faith, hope, joy, confidence, clarity, peace and purpose, it affirms the extent to which Christ uses His own as instruments of righteous reconciliation to God.

Further encouragement in the critical task of Christian evangelism, serving to refresh, renew, and rekindle its zeal, comes from the venerable Paul, apostle to the Gentiles: *"For though I am free from all men, I have made myself a slave to all,* that I might <u>win the more</u>...I have become all things to all men, that I may by all means <u>save some</u>. And I do all things for the sake of the gospel, that I may become fellow partaker of it" (1 Corinthians 9:19-23). Perhaps equal to any other verses in the New Testament, this pericope rightly interpreted and faithfully applied to present-day Christian living can inspire enhanced evangelistic engagement. Thus, they should be prayerfully considered and thoroughly examined.

The apostle Paul, in 1 Corinthians 9, demonstrated a profound inclination toward keeping score, toward measuring achievement, saying: "that I might win the more." (If Paul attended a sporting event, he would enjoy the atmosphere, time with other spectators, action on the field, etc.; but the score would be critical to him.) In regard to the advance of the kingdom, in the name of Christ, Paul aimed to win the battle against the enemy of Christ, and the enemy of the righteous. Every new convert to Christ represents a "point" on the board. The preponderance of such points means that the Christian cause yet prevails in the world.

By implication, Paul refuted Christianity cloistered in the sanctuary. Rather, in aiming to "win some," he took Christ to the streets. Truly, as the focus of the Christian faith transcended the sacred space of the sanctuary, as Christians "talk Him up" among humanity, God delights to usher in a mighty manifestation of His will. Indeed, God "desires all men to be saved and to come to the knowledge of the truth" (1 Timothy 2:4). Indisputably, that truth is personified in Christ Jesus alone.

What, then, could Paul teach us, as he pursued the lost?

1) There are hordes of lost people in the world.

In Paul's day, there were three distinct groups of lost humanity to which he directed special evangelistic attention: 1) Jews, under the Law; 2) Gentiles, without the Law; and, 3) the "weak." His objective, strategy, and tactics aligned with the group with whom he sought to share Christ as Savior. No matter what, Paul wanted to "win some."

If it meant adhering to Jewish Law and their religious sensibilities, Paul would acquiesce so as to present the Christian Gospel to them. If it meant viewing life through the prism of the Gentiles, with scholarship, appeals to wisdom, and a sense of the uniqueness of Christ, Paul was prepared to meet them, in order to present the Christian Gospel. Finally, if it meant finding a point of accommodation with those ensnared in sin, thus, "weak" in their understanding, Paul would then usher them into the powerful presence of Christ the Savior. Indeed, his entire "modus operandi" involved developing a psychic connection and deep kinship with diverse humanity, without judgment, but on the basis of divine grace, so as to, ultimately "win some."

Today, we should heed Paul's model, knowing there are still lost, unsaved people among us. The nature of the lost and the unsaved varies with the individuals. Some are suave, successful, charismatic, and enthusiastic; yet, they are lost. Some are broken, bruised, and battered by life; yet, they are lost. Some are promiscuous and profane; again, they are lost. Some are prone to alcohol and drugs; so, we affirm their lost condition.

Indeed, Christians must meet the unsaved where they may be found, without acting in the same way as the unsaved.

Others are lost, while quite influential in journalistic, academic, corporate, political, entertainment, and athletic sectors. Others are lost as suburban "stay-at-home" moms, or golf-playing dads. Others are lost, navigating urban ghettoes and barrios. Others are lost on college campuses and on university faculties. Others are lost on the stage, the screen, the diamond, and before millions.

Today, no matter where lost people are emotionally or psychically, we know that, fundamentally, their malady lies in the inherent sin nature. So, we love people, despite their sinfulness, with divine grace. We call them, however, to a higher moral and ethical standard through Christ. We follow the lead of our Savior: *"Now all the tax-gatherers and the sinners were coming near Him to listen to Him. And both the Pharisees and the scribes began to grumble, saying, 'This man receives sinners and eats with them'"* (Luke 15:1-2). As Christ's severest critics speak of His compassion for sinners, they affirm the uniqueness of His calling: *"to seek and to save that which was lost"* (Luke 19:10).

Often, I ask our congregants: "Are the unsaved comfortable around you?" Most saints I know evince a desire to avoid, at all costs, the profane, the loud, the uncouth, and the "worldly," fearing that such persons will remind them of former days in the lost condition. Here is my response: as the *"light of the world"* (Matthew 5:14), Christians have, through the indwelling Holy Spirit of God, the power to dispel the darkness. And, in dispelling that darkness with the light of Christ, the unsaved will *"see your good works, and glorify your Father who is in heaven"* (Matthew 5:16). That is why personal Christian evangelism really matters!

2) Christians seeking evangelistic engagement must meet intellectual, personal, biblical, and spiritual challenges.

When the objective involves "winning some" to Christ, saints of God should prepare for a long siege against the enemy. Often, many lost persons will agree to the biblical terms of salvation, but will then hesitate when it comes to making a decision. Others may affirm the need for a closer walk with God, knowing Christ as absolutely, *"the way, and the truth, and the life, with no one coming to the Father, but through Him"* (John 14:6). Even with that foundation, some will falter and procrastinate.

An illustration of this human proclivity to stall in meaningful moments might aid our discussion. Years ago, I visited a car dealer. The salesman asked what I might be interested in purchasing. I told him my vehicular preference. After seeing that specific vehicle (loaded with preferred amenities), and two hours of discussion, I said I would come back another day, when I was "ready." Finally, perhaps exasperated by my stalling tactics, he asked: "Sir, what will it take to get you to purchase an automobile?" Only then did I make the purchase. Something in the human condition resists making a commitment until one is demanded.

As dedicated Christian disciples, saints of God must lovingly, sincerely, and firmly, press the unsaved toward making a life-transforming, supernatural, eternal commitment to Jesus Christ as Savior. Every time the Gospel is presented, an accompanying "must" is inherent. Consider Peter's Pentecost preaching, with its implicit invitation to engagement: *"Now when they heard this, they were pierced to the heart, and said to Peter and the rest of the apostles, 'Brethren, what shall we do?'"* (Acts 2:37). Immediately, the response from Peter was succinct: *"Repent, and let each of you be baptized in the name of Jesus Christ for the forgiveness of your sins..."* (Acts 2:38).

Safe conjecture leads us to the conclusion that, without an assertive proclamation of the Christian message, thousands would have left worship on the Day of Pentecost without making a firm commitment to Christ and His developing body of disciples. A strong Christ-centered message, followed by a confident invitation to join Christ, produces positive results, expanding the kingdom of God.

3) Christ is central to the evangelistic endeavor; results will be left to the insight, perfect timing, and absolute direction of God's Holy Spirit.

If saints of God over-emphasize reaching the unsaved to join their particular church fellowship, to follow their favorite minister, to share in their denomination, or to embrace their theological interpretation, the result will be disappointment, fruitlessness, and failure. Human-centered Christianity inevitably fails to reach millions. On the other hand, as Christ serves as the ultimate attraction in reaching the unsaved, the result will be forgiveness, salvation, fulfillment, peace, and joy unspeakable.

While I heartily celebrate contemporary "praise" music, I yet respect traditional hymns. *"Lift Him Up"* summarizes my thesis on the centrality of Christ for personal salvation:

> *"How to reach the masses, men of ev'ry birth, for an answer Jesus gave the key: 'And I, if I be lifted up from the earth, will draw all men unto Me.' Oh! The world is hungry for the Living Bread, lift the Savior up for them to see; Trust Him, and do not doubt the words that He said, 'I'll draw all men unto me.' Lift Him up, Lift Him up, still He speaks from eternity: 'And I, if I be lifted up from the earth, will draw all men unto Me."*

In Paul's' formulation in 1 Corinthians 9, he evidenced a desperate yearning, compelling him to great lengths in reaching the lost. Today, too often, if saints of God "go witnessing," it involves a time-defined venture, rather than one that might require some stress and strain, before another yields to the promptings of God's Holy Spirit.

Again, in the battle for the souls of the lost, we must never expect the enemy to relent at the first presentation of the Gospel message: *"For our struggle is not against flesh and blood, but against the rulers, against the world forces of this darkness, against the spiritual forces of wickedness in the heavenly places"* (Ephesians 6:12). The believer's enemies are the demonic hosts of Satan, hell-bent on preventing the unsaved from positively responding to the grace of God, in sending Christ as Savior to liberate all from sin. In light of the tremendous change we have experienced because of Christ, that fact alone should embolden us to take that message to the masses. Encountering obstacles (doubt, hostility, ridicule) are part of the strategy of the demonic.

4) The unsaved will hide behind any façade, to avoid facing their lost condition.

Within our text under examination, 1 Corinthians 9:19-23, Paul seized the initiative, proudly presenting the glorious truth of salvation through Christ. With intention, he went *"to the Jews, to those without law, and to the weak,"* fully persuaded that the Christ message potentially produces internal cleansing, transformation of outlook, and restoring of hope, while offering spiritual liberty.

Often, I think the current Christian malady is a simple one: too many expect the unsaved masses to come to saints, asking, "Will you please tell me about Christ?" From my experience, the yearning may be in the individual, but access to the remedy flows from the one certain of its benefit. In the illustration I cited above, the car salesman knew I wanted (and he wanted me) to purchase an automobile. He simply had to convince me of the necessity of the sale in that moment. The fact that he successfully sent me home in an automobile speaks to his ability as a salesman. Fearful of stretching this analogy too far, more Christians need to "sell" (evangelize) ready buyers (lost sinners) our "product" (salvation through Christ).

5) Paul is recognized as the foremost spokesman for the spread of the Christian cause, pursuing it with a resolute heart.

In that spirit, I recently challenged our congregation to affirm what should represent our highest priority in service to God. Reasonably, some said it should be high, spirited worship of God. Others said it should embody living a sanctified, character-filled life for Christ. Others held that it should be seen in the daily acquisition of biblical knowledge. Others felt it should be cultivating a strong prayer life. Others argued for social justice as the prime responsibility of the Christian movement. On we went in debating the merits of various Christian emphases. Sadly, few felt Christians should "plant their flag," demonstrating obedience to Christ's call for worldwide evangelism.

Faced with this, I felt the leading of God to begin an extensive church Bible study teaching on the subject of Christian evangelism. No Christian pastor or denominational leader should assume that individual saints understand the ultimate priority of Jesus Christ, especially if they have not been taught it! And, owing to changes in emphases in the Christian world, some of us will have to teach the subject again to this generation of believers.

Therefore, for the widest possible impact, I sensed confirmation in affirming the central thesis of this book: every saint of God must share His love through Christ, for humanity's salvation.

The overriding zeal for Christ evangelism today must be firmly rooted in compassionate concern for the plight of unsaved humanity. Recognizing people's lost condition that of facing eternity without Christ—should hasten evangelistic engagement.

We take vital clues from the attitude of the apostle Paul, reflecting on the obstinate state of the Jews of his day: *"Brethren, my heart's desire and prayer to God for them is for their salvation. For I bear them witness that they have zeal for God, but not in accordance with knowledge. For not knowing about God's righteousness, and seeking to establish their own, they did not subject themselves to the righteousness of God. For Christ is the end of the law for righteousness to everyone who believes"* (Romans 10:1-4).

This Romans 10 passage is quite instructive, starting with what it does not reveal. First, Paul was not there advocating political liberation, even as the Jews chafed under Roman oppression. Second, he was not encouraging economic enhancement as the antidote for their anguish. Third, he was not promoting higher social status in society. Instead, Paul went to the very core of their need: spiritual transformation through Jesus Christ.

Further, Paul stressed that the Jews' zeal, lacking a necessary Christ-basis, had led them to *"establish their own righteousness"* (seen today in alternative religions, superstitions, haughtiness, and claiming "spirituality" without Christ). Evangelistic engagement in American culture is made all the more difficult because many unsaved persons erect elaborate facades to hide their hurt. Instead, they should "drop the mask," repenting of their sins, while asking Christ to become Savior and Lord of their lives.

Finally, today, vast groups of unsaved humanity (among every race and ethnicity, gender, class, and condition) need at its core a living faith in the Savior of the world, Jesus Christ. Weep, we must, for those mired in the muck of yesterday's failures, unsure of God's forgiveness and release from guilt. Unsure, many cower in silent emotional incarceration, trying just about any pseudo-remedy (drugs, alcohol, multiple tattoos, "hook-ups," entertainment, sports and nihilism) for dulling their internal pain.

When astute Christian leaders, theologians, and congregants truly discern the cultural landscape, observing the spiritual vacuum engulfing so many, we quickly come to realize the grand scale of unsaved angst. As I have stated elsewhere in these pages, external changes (hair, eyes, fashion, jewelry, or "things") cannot assuage long-term, internal pain. For that, everyone needs the ultimate panacea: Christ Jesus as Savior.

So, zeal for shouting out God's grace in Christ (evangelism) increases in direct proportion to the level of pain I view every day. Mass murders, inhumanity, perversion, cheapened life, corruption, embezzlement, bullying, Ponzi schemes, domestic violence, political graft, family degradation, moral confusion, and more demand a godly response. I, for one, am tired of watching the news, reading the news, or scanning the Internet without seeing the need for mass evangelism in the name of the Savior. Indeed, Christ represents the world's only hope!

CHAPTER 8

Resources to Strengthen Christian Evangelism

Up to this point, I pray that this work has served to whet the appetite of those yearning for a return to Christian evangelism as the central pillar in the overall Christian mission today. Christianity, in short, involves drawing, wooing, persuading, and leading the unsaved to the Savior, for the express purpose of expanding the kingdom of God. My plea throughout this book has been a simple one: to mobilize the full body of Christ toward one-on-one soul-winning among unbelievers. In some quarters, this position is referred to as "evangelical" Christianity; for me, it is simply radical obedience to the Great Commission of Christ, articulated in Matthew 28:18-20, which enjoins saints of God to "make disciples" of all nations.

A long-time, dear friend, Bishop Kenneth Ulmer of Los Angeles, holds that: *"Evangelism is ministering light in a dark world. When you love people through evangelism, you serve them and give them the thing they need most: the truth about who Jesus is and who He can be to them. Evangelism is finding*

God's lost sheep. It is binding up the broken ones and feeding the hungry ones. Evangelism is the purest form of ministry because it requires a heart that loves Jesus enough to tell the truth about Him and loves another enough to bring Him home at all cost."

I wholeheartedly concur with Ulmer's assessment on Christian evangelism. We should pray that other national Christian leaders express a similar passion for the unsaved among us. If the lost are to hear glorious truth regarding Christ, such that would transform lives, it must come from the lips of the saved. I am an unabashed advocate for a simple principle and proposition: *"Let the redeemed of the Lord say so"* (Psalm 107:2).

Passion for lost souls to discover spiritual transformation through Christ is never "out of season," nor should it represent an intermittent theme of certain leaders, groups, or congregations. None should be dissuaded from evangelistic engagement, nor intimidated by the enemy, feeling that evangelism is judgmental, intolerant or offensive. Instead, the total Christian family should embrace the liberating message of Christ toward a lost, confused, fragmented, dying world of humanity, as He alone is its supreme hope.

In many ways, Christians resemble a medical doctor with the only known cure for a virulent, contagious illness afflicting a vast populace. It would repudiate medical ethics, as well as the "Hippocratic oath," bordering on malpractice, if such a healing professional refused to give needy patients this medicine. Likewise, when Christian disciples view the unsaved around us, it should compel us to share the only effective "medicine" (truth in Christ Jesus) with the "sick" in our midst (those ensnared in immorality, indifference, and indecision). To do otherwise undermines saints' adherence to the central mission of Christianity: making Christian disciples for the kingdom of God.

The reason I take a bold stance in confronting individuals in sinful alienation from God, denying Christ as Savior, yet calling them to repentance and faith, stems from my divine calling as a Christian preacher. Fundamentally, I exist to bring new people to salvation through the blood of Jesus. None can deter me from being a consummate soul-winner, as I know my reason for being, my ultimate purpose in life: to serve as an instrument of divine grace, mercy, and love, exemplified in Jesus Christ.

Those who share my sense of divine calling to Christian ministry might similarly affirm the necessity of wide deployment of the body of Christ to the lost in our midst. Everywhere we look, God has potential converts for His kingdom: in the mall, in the gym, on the school campus, on the golf course, in the courtroom, in corporate suites, on the job site, at the bank, in the post office, in the cleaners, in the barbershop, and in the coffee house.

Recently, our city witnessed a deadly domestic-violence scenario, resulting in the murder of a young mother, allegedly at the hands of her live-in mate, the father of their four children. While her family grieves in a way none can share, I also grieve, wondering if she had accepted Christ as her personal Savior. Perhaps, we can only hope for the best. Yet, her brief life span twenty-seven years, should remind all Christians of the importance of sharing the message of salvation through Christ with all. It must become more than cliché: we never know the length of our days. Fittingly, then, we must ascertain another's spiritual standing before God. "Old-school" Christianity was quite bold: "Do you know Christ as your personal Savior?" Yes, that's blunt! Yet, it gets at the most significant issue of life.

Every city in America has similar stories of young lives lost, whether by drug abuse, domestic disputes, gang warfare, suicides, school rampages, or an array of other, senseless tragedies. After the media departs and the hoopla dissipates, Christians should examine the devastation left in their wake. People really matter to God; and God sent His only Son to earth, with one objective: to reconcile alienated humanity to the heavenly Father.

If more Christians expect successful outcomes in evangelistic engagement, they will need ample resources for the task. Following are a few enumerated resources available to would-be evangelists: biblical principles, theological reflection, practical teaching, rigorous training, evangelism literature, articles, tape series, mission conferences, strategy sessions, preaching emphases, technological assets, networking and more. These resources are available to every Christian leader, congregation, theologian, and denominational leader. When we implement these resources, starting at the local congregational level, coursing through theological seminaries/Bible colleges, and ascending to national denominational curricula, we may see the Christian Gospel gain an invaluable "beachhead" in the minds and the hearts of millions in America and globally.

Of course, resources, like tools, are only valuable when used by those aiming to construct something of long-term utility. In the parlance of corporate culture, many refer to using everything in one's "tool kit." In my mind, the Christian church should at all times examine its "tools" on the principle of utility: Are these spiritual tools assets for the objective we have in mind? Let us evaluate some tools, or resources, available for reaching the unsaved.

1) A Christian testimony

One of the great resources at the disposal of all Christians involves our testimony of what God did for us, bringing us to salvation. Such a testimony should direct all praise to God for cleansing, forgiving, saving, and owning us as His children. In every way, we should make it clear that our transformation was made possible solely through the shed blood of Jesus, from the cross of Calvary. The vicarious death of Christ pays our sin debt. Now, that's "old-school" theology; but, it is still true!

In our local Christian fellowship, I celebrate and encourage persons coming from sensate, sordid, sin-filled pasts, filled with alcohol, drugs, promiscuity and more, sharing Christ's intervention, to testify of their new lives of faith. Of course, such a transformative testimony might require some caution, leaving out explicit details and omitting the names of other persons involved. I have two thoughts associated with the power of testimony: 1) Various "12-step" programs (AA, Narc-anon) include this feature; and, 2) The apostle Paul in the New Testament made his personal testimony central to radical obedience in Christ.

Lost people need to know that God's power is not hindered by rash, un-enlightened, ill-considered decisions and foolish acts. Into this quagmire of sin, Christ comes to set all things right: *"But God demonstrates His own love toward us, in that while we were yet sinners, Christ died for us"* (Romans 5:8).

Perhaps I watch the wrong Christian television broadcasts, because what I hear from certain quarters of the Christian faith community seems great for believers: healing, breakthrough, authority over the enemy, fundamentals of a great marriage, walking in prosperity (materialism), obtaining keys to dynamic faith, launching a business, writing a novel, etc.

At the same time, I don't hear enough of what Christ can do for sinners: cleanse them from guilt and shame, make righteous, promise rest in glory, seat them in heavenly places, endow them with the power of the Holy Spirit, and show them the excellence of God's awesome grace. Christians, in my view, need to dust the cobwebs off our testimonies of God's grace in Christ.

As the Christian faith today is portrayed as godly folks enjoying exclusive benefits, it becomes akin to an exclusive "club" for special people. Increasingly, the current generation of saints substitute "club" for "hospital" as the metaphor for Christ's mission. Yet, Christ clearly articulated His saving emphasis, His primary concern: *"It is not those who are healthy who need a physician, but those who are sick; I did not come to call the righteous, but sinners"* (Mark 2:17). Sinners, I would submit, were central to the heart of God in Christ; and, today, sinners should still be central to the heart of God's saints.

A further deficit of current Christianity, in my view, is its alignment with a "middle-class" American perspective, while much of the world cannot relate to the emphases of an earlier paragraph (crass consumer commercialism). In short, Christ gave His life for more than striving Christians' ability to own expensive vehicles, live in exclusive neighborhoods, wear designer/custom-tailored apparel, bank thousands monthly, enjoy pensions, and anticipate exotic vacations, with few overt cares. None of this makes sense, as millions around the globe are mired in poverty, denied freedoms under brutal political regimes, unable to enjoy pleasures, with little hope for better days. Into this mix, however, we present the redeeming Christ!

Irrespective of locale, region, or nation, Christ "sets humanity free," from hopelessness, from sins of the past, from aimlessness, from defeat, from existential despair, and from all that constricts us. Too often, lost people are victims of the consequences of their lust, pride, selfishness, senseless brutality, and capricious sense of violence. Deeply unhappy with their lives, emotionally depleted, lacking a spiritual remedy, they wallow in sin. False bravado causes many unsaved to rebuff attempts to bring them to saving faith in Christ. Dedicated saints, moved by evangelistic zeal, must fervently pray that God will "break down" the walls, as His Holy Spirit destroys "chains."

2) Christians must properly evaluate their communities.

The Christian witness, in its many dimensions, locales, and ethnicities, must contend with another challenge: the rise of the religiously unaffiliated. By this I mean, millions claim faith in Christ, but they choose to express it outside His body, cut off from regular corporate worship, disassociated from other believers, and adrift from loving congregations. The Pew Research Center, while studying this phenomenon for its implications for the Roman Catholic Church and its relations with Hispanics, also aids the full body of Christ, as we evaluate effective evangelistic strategies for winning the lost to Christ.

In reference to religious demographics, researchers speak of "faith-switching" (from Catholicism to Protestantism, particularly to Pentecostalism). They cannot fathom that some would repudiate their parents' faith for a faith of their own. However, millions do this all the time. Today, persons seek Christianity because it challenges them through a personal God to embrace Christ as an alive, engaged Savior. They also see the Bible as authoritative principles for living, offering fulfillment in a relationship of divine faith. Even Christian music facilitates this search: praise songs are directed to God, rather than simply being about Him.

Everything I am writing here involves fostering Christian evangelism toward top-of-mind recognition among saints of God, especially Christian leaders, theologians, congregations and denominational executives. When we target those who have the power to "set the agenda" for the work of the people of God, we gain traction in reaching the lost with Christ's message of ultimate hope. Far from simply enjoying saved status, I am calling for reorientation in thought, as to what it means to be Christian in the twenty-first century. In my view, it means being passionate about faith in Christ, to the extent that it is utterly repugnant to keep such joy, gladness, peace, and favor to ourselves. Instead, all that Christ has done for those "in the beloved," must be shared, so that unsaved others may likewise enjoy the advantages of new life in Christ.

3) Christian leaders share responsibility for evangelism engagement.

Another critical resource for "scalability" (making Christian evangelism the central thrust of the Christian witness) requires national thought-leaders to spearhead the effort. As many Christian leaders take cues from successful Christian leaders, I am prayerful that the Spirit of God will use national Christian voices to call more of us to our core mission: making disciples. Since words are elastic, with many arguing semantics, I need to define what "making disciples" means to me: teaching the saved to love God, honor Him, obey Him, and walk in fellowship with Him, all because of salvation in Christ. Also, such disciples will intentionally seek to lead others to the Savior.

For a long time, local Christian leaders and congregations have been expected to fulfill the mission of Christ. While I heartily applaud the work of the body of Christ in its most immediate connection to humanity, I also expect leadership from and dialogue with Christian seminaries and Bible colleges, as students in them are being groomed as thought-leaders for the present and future generations. While considering matriculation in its Doctor of Ministry program, I was moved by the mission statement of Central Baptist Theological Seminary in Kansas. *This Christian institution aims to prepare students to transform churches and communities by educating and forming them as Christian leaders who are biblically knowledgeable, theologically articulate, spiritually healthy, humanly sensitive, and culturally competent.*

I am sure that other such schools in America operate from a similar perspective. As they produce such scholars, the result will be greater engagement in the central mission of the church of the Lord Jesus Christ in the twenty-first century. Indeed, we need their guidance in focusing the attention of graduates on that which our Savior made the cornerstone of ministry: "to seek and to save the lost" (Luke 19:10). As seminaries and Bible colleges fervently promote personal evangelism, the entire body of Christ benefits. More saints of God will be deployed to reach the unsaved with the Christian Gospel.

At the same time, I am well aware of the fact that not all Christian leaders (irrespective of race, ethnicity, gender, class, or locale) will embrace theological education from an accredited seminary or Bible college. Truly, many Christian leaders, past and present, have been dedicated servants of God, who, for a variety of reasons, were not or are not seminary-trained. However, with the current explosion of knowledge through technology and online learning, there is really no acceptable basis for not receiving critical insight from the Word of God.

4) Secular power illustrates the necessity of extolling Christ.

In seeking to marshal all available resources for Christian evangelism, I am reminded of the way America exerts its power in a massive war effort: American ground troops, air assaults, tanks, heavy weapons, leadership, special-forces, military intelligence, and more are brought to bear. Similarly, we need the finest, sharpest minds, honed in theological academies, able to assist local pastors and congregations, grappling with the challenges of twenty-first century skepticism, a secular mindset, and a refusal to embrace the supernatural in Jesus Christ.

My concern is production of "critical mass," as the total thrust of the Christian church returns to compassion for the lost condition of all humanity. While saints of God have never fully jettisoned Christian evangelism intellectually or practically, the last few decades have seen it eclipsed as the preeminent concern of God's church. This is, indeed, a tragedy!

When and where thousands of Christians gather around one concept—evangelism—it will focus our attention on the ultimate calling of Christ. In the last fifty years, large numbers of Christians have rallied to promote many vital causes (social justice, disaster relief, ending abortion, nuclear disarmament, racial peace, women's equality, preaching, church growth, youth engagement, and more). Perhaps it is high time we return to our first century calling: getting new converts to Christ. Indeed, God's indictment of His church should be clear: *"But I have this against you, that you have left your first love"* (Revelation 2:4).

Theologians and biblical scholars are left with perhaps two interpretations of the object of this "first-love" reference. Either the people have willfully abandoned God, or they have forsaken the priority of God. Either way, the unsaved have been forgotten in the process. Today, this "first-love" notion should be thoroughly examined, as the number one priority of the Christian witness should embody loving God and loving humanity, in the name of a loving, gracious, patient God.

5) Changed lives will exhilarate Christian evangelism.

At the congregational level, I pray that a mighty move of God will usher in greater concern for the lost, primarily through preaching and teaching from the pulpits of every conceivable gathering of saints. Rather than more "feel-good" sermons, lacking a mission responsibility, what if we heard more of the Christian mandate to bring the lost to the Master? When we replace "paralytic" with "unsaved," we capture evangelistic zeal: *"And they came, bringing to Him a paralytic, carried by four men"* (Mark 2:3). As stated earlier, the unsaved in our midst are sick, not with a physical ailment, but with a spiritual one. The great challenge of Christian evangelism involves bringing "them" to Him, for He alone possesses power to eternally alter their destiny.

6) Where are the national Christian evangelism conferences?

In the last few decades, millions of Christians have flocked to every kind of conference: expository preaching, church growth, prayer, denominational, and more. Some of these, let us be honest, have been excuses for Christian ministers and influential lay leaders to "get away," under the guise of feeding mind, heart and will, for the advancement of the kingdom of God.

Moreover, a forgotten resource for fostering Christian evangelism involves a structured, well-designed evangelism/mission conference. In it, all the plenary speakers and workshop leaders would emphasize various aspects of the topic. Also, they could present printed materials and Power-point slides, with specific Scriptures for targeted audiences. Especially in smaller workshops, participants could "role-play," raising and meeting the inevitable excuses and rationales of the unsaved.

Over the course of my nearly 40-year Christian ministry, I have attended several national evangelism conferences. In candor, they were sponsored by white congregations or white denominations. Unfortunately, I cannot recall hearing of, let alone attending, such a national one, from the black Christian perspective, ever!

7) A Christian denominational imperative

In this regard, I must affirm that the Southern Baptist Convention—despite an ugly history supporting slavery, encouraging discrimination, upholding Jim Crow segregation, while for decades excluding African-Americans—yet champions evangelism as its first priority! In my judgment, they still have substantial work to do in "social justice." They err in aligning themselves with the political right in determined defiance of

America's first black president. SBC should receive high marks for ecclesiological success, while getting barely passing ones for true social justice engagement. Yet, I am optimistic for them, viewing changes made so far, with every expectation of greater improvements in the future. Every Christian entity (Anglo, African-American, Latino, and Asian) possesses the power to change, grow, and better relate to its continuing challenges.

While prodding the SBC and other notable Christian groups toward greater appreciation of diversity, inclusion, and the need for compassion for America's impoverished, black Christians can learn from those groups committed to Christ's mission of reaching the unsaved, especially in developing creative, effective ways to implement evangelism. The life and work of individual Christian saints and local congregations suffers to the degree that we neglect seeking the lost. Indeed, good strategies and tactics should never be regarded by source, but rather by adherence to Scripture and utility. With regular baptisms and numerical increase as indices of effectiveness, we should applaud all godly means of reaching the lost with the message of Christ.

Admittedly, I am a bottom-line person, a pragmatist. I start from the premise of, "Is this taking me toward or away from my goal?" If I conclude that the matter is of significance, I wholeheartedly embrace it. On the other hand, if I conclude that the undertaking is foolish, empty, and pointless, I quickly drop it. Emotional attachment only makes sense if I deem the matter critical to life. Since I have a brief life-span, I yearn to dedicate all the time God has given me to things in alignment with advancement of the kingdom of God through Jesus Christ. I operate from a sobering life-principle: "You are just a vapor that appears for a little while and then vanishes away" (James 4:14).

8) Christian leaders must "lead" in Christian evangelism, above other interests.

For this reason, I suppose, I have few hobbies. Sorry, but I don't golf. Aside from a select group of professional golfers, most will never rise to golf legend. (Civil-rights leader Dr. Martin Luther King Jr. was not primarily known as a golfer, though he may have been one.) People must find what for and where they will make a mark. Indeed, one becomes proficient in what one practices. Yet, every saint of God can have unusual attainment as a soul-winner, reaching the unsaved, provided we give it similar devotion, dedication, and discipline.

At the same time, I don't frequent gyms or health clubs, though friends suggest that I should. (I do, however, strenuously watch my diet.) In a greater way, I am convicted by Paul's words: *"Discipline yourself for the purpose of godliness; for bodily discipline is only of little profit, but godliness is profitable for all things, since it holds promise for the present life and also for the life to come"* (1 Timothy 4:7-8).

9) Christian leaders, as with all leaders, will be measured by their objectives.

In the final analysis, as boring as it seems, I have dedicated my waking moments and fleeting years to that which brings ultimate glory to the heavenly Father: bringing new persons to saving faith in the risen Savior. Primarily, I achieve this evangelistic objective through preaching, teaching, one-on-one sharing, leading, writing, and conveying the rudiments of a soul-winning curriculum.

Like Steve Jobs or Bill Gates (computers/software), Michael Jordan or Lebron James (basketball), Warren Buffett or Charles Schwab (investments), Lyndon Johnson or Ronald Reagan (politics), Pablo Picasso (portrait art), Albert Einstein (physics), Sigmund Freud (psychiatric research), Bob Hope or Johnny Carson (comedy), Dwight Eisenhower or Douglass McArthur (military tactics), Billy Graham or E.V. Hill (soul-winning preaching), all must sense legacy-building while yet alive.

The only way to ensure such an enduring legacy, in whatever discipline, requires giving the task one's full focus, one's all, for as long as one lives. As always, we affirm the New Testament exemplar of this truth: *"Paul began devoting himself completely to the word, solemnly testifying to the Jews that Jesus was the Christ"* (Acts 18:5b). Indeed, I sincerely pray to "make my mark" as a saint wholly dedicated to Christian evangelism.

10) Christian evangelism will be fostered by technology.

The final resource available to Christians in the early twenty-first century, which fosters evangelism, involves wide usage of new and emerging technology. This notion represents a recurring theme that I refer to throughout this book. We can safely assert that never in human history have there been so many ways to connect with others. Information moves at the speed of light. We can instantly access new sources of information. Indeed, globalization makes close neighbors of seven billion who inhabit the planet. The only limitations to an online presence for an innovative, progressive Christian congregation are creativity, taste, propriety, and willingness to remain current with world trends. Wise Christian leaders will examine every way possible to use technology to reach the unsaved, with the cleansing, saving, hope-filled message of Jesus Christ.

Practically, then, every local Christian congregation must develop its own Web site. It should provide clear, useful, easy-to-access information for any seeker: church history, biblical beliefs, pastoral leadership, staff, worship times, site directions, upcoming events, and more. This vital information should clearly express that congregation's unique vision to serve humanity in the name of the risen Christ. A Web site alone will signal to the larger community, city, state, nation and world, that congregation's willingness to reach beyond its sanctuary for new souls for the kingdom of God.

Further, in light of many Christ-followers using texts, e-mails, Facebook pages, YouTube videos, Twitter hashtags, Instagram presence, blogs, with capacity for online navigation, more saints of God could use these social-media venues to share their faith in Christ. As a suggestion, persons so inclined could mention their church names, recent sermon topics, major insights from the message, the plan of salvation, favorite Scriptures, and prayers, among discussion items; rather than trivial, mundane, inane ecclesiological gossip. Indeed, as more online profiles become Christ-centered, it may drive some silly "friends" away. (That's a blessing!) Conversely, the unsaved may be led to Christ as a result of your enthusiasm regarding the Savior and His church. In short, for a believer, everything should focus faith in Christ.

For those frightened by or unfamiliar with the terminology, functions, intricacies and opportunities of the Internet or social media, I challenge all to learn. Technology is here; and, it will only increase its usages and efficiencies. None can hide from its growing impact. Instead, we can take solace in "dummies" like me. (If I can learn technology, everyone can!) Truly, if the body of Christ wishes to faithfully represent our Savior, as His "ambassadors" (2 Corinthians 5:20), we must know and function in the language of those we expect to reach with truth centered in Christ.

11) **Embrace technology, without denying "old" media in reaching the unsaved.**

While I champion "new" media, in the quest to share the grace of God embodied in Christ, I also appreciate "old" means of evangelistic outreach: radio, television, "snail-mail," revivals, crusades, newspapers, billboards, and signs.

Indeed, when the objective involves the widest possible dissemination of Christ's message to a decaying, deteriorating, dying culture, we should adopt every means at our disposal. Extensive, creative, innovative evangelistic outreach emerges from a bedrock biblical principle: *"I have become all things to all men, so that I may by all means save some"* (1 Corinthians 9:22).

Often, I wonder: *"Is the Church of Jesus Christ in the twenty-first century really using this "all-means" rubric to reach this generation for the advancement of the kingdom of God?"* If so, there will be tangible results from fervent outreach to the unsaved, in the name of our Savior. If not, Christian leaders and congregations will remain mired in complacency and mediocrity, with negligible gains for God's kingdom. In Christian ministry, I have witnessed a mystery wrapped in an enigma, culminating in a deep paradox: How is it that one congregation in a community or a city thrives, while another one in the same locale shrivels up? Indeed, tying the answer to the sovereignty of God, or that,

"Every church will not become a mega-church," might make some feel better; yet, it may be the lament of the lazy.

Please observe my reasoning: If the Master said the *"harvest is plentiful,"* (Matthew 9:37), then why are so few congregations experiencing an abundant harvest? Could the answer reside in the same text? Note the Lord's instruction: *"Therefore beseech the Lord of the harvest to send out workers into His harvest"* (Matthew 9:38). So, this book seeks to deliberately mobilize and then to deploy more "workers" for a promised harvest of souls. It's that simple, and that profound. It's the mission of the Master in a mere moment.

Relative to all the resources available to the body of Christ expressed in this chapter, the objective has been clearly and wonderfully mandated by Christ: convey the redemptive message of Christ to unsaved masses, everywhere they may be found. Saints, thus, utilize every available method toward that end. Through the agency of God's Holy Spirit, persons are then regenerated and begin their life-long journey of Christian discipleship.

CHAPTER 9

Varied Evangelism Approaches

In advancing the notion of Christian evangelism, one comes quickly to the conclusion that the approach to the unsaved is as important as the content of the presentation. In other words, we must adapt the approach (without in any way compromising the Gospel message centered in Jesus Christ) to fit the targeted person or group. For example, as is oft-stated, in 1 Corinthians 9:19-23, the apostle Paul, in the context of aiming to reach new converts for Christ among diverse groups, considered multiple factors in evangelistic strategy. To the Jewish community, Paul would tailor his message to their sensibilities: adherence to the law given by Moses. Simultaneously, to others not under the Jewish law, Paul approached them differently. Equally true, to those referred to as "weak," he would present an entirely different set of propositions. The common truth was (and still is) that in Christ every person and group discovers real, redemptive and rich life before God the Father.

Today, faced with a "post-modern" generation (those typically unmoored from traditional considerations of morality, ethics, limits or restraints), the Christian faith community must grapple with the proper approach in reaching them with the claims of the Christ-centered Gospel. Again, I repeat: in no way should saints of God compromise the biblical principles of salvation through the convicting power and regenerative effect of the Holy Spirit of God. All must affirm the vicarious death and bodily resurrection of the Savior, Jesus Christ.) Christian methods must expand according to the needs of the targeted audience, while maintaining a consistent Christian message. That "tension" and "balance" must characterize the contemporary Christian outreach to the unsaved among us.

Further, the demographics between the ages of 18-34 might be termed the "connected-but-distracted" generation. With every known technological advance at its disposal, this cohort lives with social media, instant access to Internet information, and many exhibit a propensity for keeping heads down to check devices, even with a "friend" sitting just across the table. Popular cultural references fill their lives: Google hangouts, Facebook town-halls, Instagram messages, Twitter tweets, and new Websites crowd their mental space. Increasingly, this generation takes its cultural prompts from MTV, BET, Univision, various networks, popular films, reality-television scenarios, comedians, and viral You Tube videos.

The growing challenge from the Christian faith community involves designing creative, innovative, persuasive means to convey the saving message of Christ to this generation. In fact, there is a key question to figure out: *"How do we share Christ with a generation lacking a conceptual framework of personal sin, moral depravity, or alienation from the eternal God?"*

Trying to grapple with reaching this "techno-centric" generation, some Christian leaders and Christian congregations have, in my view, jettisoned critical, foundational touchstones. Christian worship, preaching emphases, length of worship, attire, music, and more have been fundamentally transformed. Over the last decade, in attempts to reach those operating by a complex technological "code," that needs to be broken, many Christian groups searched in vain. While I applaud the attempt, I caution against "twisting-like-a-pretzel," to reach persons who need bedrock truth: *"Jesus said to him, 'I am the way, and the truth, and the life; no one comes to the Father, but through Me'"* (John 14:6).

In our church fellowship in Kansas City, we have tried to lift a vision for the next generation built on the foundation of Christ, through dynamic worship, utilizing technology, with youth leading in key places. Indeed, they know that world quite well. Over the years, also, we have experimented with conveying the Christian message through rap, up-tempo music, retreats, and special youth fellowship gatherings. Further, we emphasize prayer before God, fasting, Bible study series, sharing faith, and giving to the kingdom of God through tithes and offerings. Finally, we lay a strong foundation on college/university life, recognizing quality academic preparation as the absolute priority for all expecting lasting professional attainment.

A word for the Christian faith community: although many adults are foreigners to the technological world inhabited by the next generation, we must strive to integrate all youth and young adults into the nexus of God's grace through Jesus Christ, fueling passion for the heavenly Father in glory.

In the larger arena of reaching unsaved adults, the body of Christ must assess its strategy to align with the expressed and the hidden needs of lost humanity in the early twenty-first-century world. Therefore, we should consider the wide variety of approaches/styles of Christian evangelism:

1) Personal

When the evangelistic approach is singular, it is extremely important that the soul-winner assess as many personal characteristics as possible: "What is the nature of my relationship with this person?" "Has he/she ever responded to the Christian gospel?" "Might he/she harbor some past experience with a Christian church or group?" *"Do I perceive hostility or openness to the presentation of the Gospel message?" "Might there be a better time and place for our conversation regarding Christ?" "Is God moving in this life, and, if so, how can I tell?"*

In asking these questions, no Christian should be dissuaded from approaching an unsaved or un-churched friend, neighbor, family member, co-worker (at break, at lunch, or after work hours) simply because such a topic might be seen as offensive, or might lead to an argument. Instead, remember these are the prime candidates for spiritual transformation through Christ. One-on-one Christian evangelism, in my judgment, represents the ultimate means of leading another to new life in Christ. Take note of the New Testament pattern of sharing saving truth in several critical respects: Jesus and the woman at the Sychar well (John 4:4ff); that same woman sharing with those in the city (John 4:39); the woman caught in adultery (John 8:11b); and so many more. Christ engaged them in a conversation, culminating in unique revelation, personal repentance and radical life-transformation.

In our day, I am convinced many Christians fail to evangelize others because they are "risk-averse," fearing they will be perceived as "pushy," "overly religious," "a holy-roller," or some other derisive term. None of that should matter to committed saints of God. In fact, we should celebrate the Word: *"Everyone who shall confess Me before men, I will also confess him before My Father who is in heaven"* (Matthew 10:32). I, for one, proudly affirm my allegiance with the Savior who died for my justification. Christ alone grants me access before the heavenly Father.

Indeed, the cause of Christ, advancing the kingdom of God, never benefits from spiritual covert operatives, or "CIA-type" Christians. Rather, more saints of God need to boldly identify themselves as dedicated followers of Christ. And, a great way to so identify with Him involves sharing new life in Christ with those bound in sin, alienated from a relationship with God.

Granted, it takes courage, daring, and confidence, to speak forth the central truth of one's Christian life. Yet, amid so many coming "out-of-the-closet" regarding their sexuality, I challenge born-again saints of God to declare their ultimate allegiance, by witnessing to a lost friend, family member, neighbor, colleague, or total stranger. Let someone else know of immense joy found in Christ. It will change their lives, and yours!

2) Intellectual

An additional approach to reaching unsaved humanity with the glorious Christian Gospel might be based on intellectual appeals. Here, I speak of Christian evangelism among college students, or those with a pseudo-sophisticated, intellectual bent.

Amid so many claiming the Bible as anti-science, or lacking epistemological substance, Christians need to meet and to refute such idiocy.

Most who castigate the biblical record as anachronistic, absurd, and without scientific fact probably could not offer specific references to the chapter or verses with which they disagree. Instead, it is part of current erudition to say something along the lines of, "*I maintain a private spirituality, respecting the divine image within me; I just don't agree with 'organized religion.'*" The inability to pierce biblical revelation from God is tantamount to refuting neuroscience or astrophysics, simply because one cannot understand the depth of the matters. Rather, through intense study, one may gain appreciation for the nuances of that intellectual discipline. Likewise, persons need greater study and immersion in the Word of God, the person and work of Christ, the way of salvation, in order to appreciate all that God has already done in fostering an eternal relationship with us. Note the Word: "*But a natural man does not accept the things of the Spirit of God; for they are foolishness to him, and he cannot understand them, because they are spiritually appraised*" (1 Corinthians 2:14).

Uppermost, Christians, attempting to evangelize the intellectual community, should never dilute the simple yet profound Gospel message centered in Christ Jesus. In fact, modern intellectual challenge cannot successfully withstand the regenerating power of the Holy Spirit of God, as He convicts individuals of their need for salvation: "*And He, when He comes, will convict the world concerning sin, and righteousness, and judgment...*" (John 16:8).

At the same time, throughout history, many intellectuals have cited the Bible as a book with tremendous spiritual, moral, and ethical appeal. Within the global Roman Catholic Church, the Society of Jesus, or the Jesuits, have as their primary purpose the propagation of the Catholic faith by any means possible, in general, and, quite often, with intellectual means, in particular. Great academic institutions, among them Notre Dame and Georgetown University in America, have been deeply influenced by Jesuit intellectualism.

Moreover, debate rages as to the Christianity of America's "Founding Fathers," with many calling them adherents of "Deism." Yet, none dispute their intellectual respect for the Bible, as it greatly shaped their notions of absolute loyalty, personal freedom, human dignity, and inherent right. (Their exclusion of blacks as worthy of such lofty notions still troubles us!). These values, upon which America was founded, are still vital to its perpetuation. Indeed, after the Holy Bible, along with the Declaration of Independence and the US Constitution, global citizens have embraced moral principles within the Judeo-Christian philosophical tradition.

The take-away concept is this: Christians must take the time and effort to engage with unsaved persons bringing legitimate intellectual inquiries. In the New Testament, intellectual grappling with the lost is best viewed in Acts 17, as the apostle Paul sought to evangelize those in Athens, the citadel of philosophical and intellectual curiosity. The record of the Athenian response to the Christian message was quite mixed: ridicule, hesitation, and belief. All in all, it represented the way contemporary unsaved persons regard the central tenets of the Christian faith. Despite the responses, saints of God must persist in sharing the Christian Gospel message, offering soul-liberation from the tentacles of sin, guilt, and shame.

When, say, Christian college students seek to evangelize their peers, the effort must be bathed in prayer, asking the Holy Spirit of God to pierce through the armor of sophistication, moral relativism, negativity, and more that hampers millions from opening their hearts to God in Christ. Additionally, many secular professors provide students with intellectual scaffolding for perverse ideas, discredited ideologies, and indecent ideals. (Yet, I want all students—even Christian ones—to critically analyze such views. Then, in comparison to the unassailable Word of God, His grace and the work of Christ, students will know that the Christian perspective is infinitely better.)

A generation ago, "Campus Crusade for Christ" was built on the premise of the unfathomable potential of changing American (and global) culture through presenting Christ on thousands of college and university campuses. Converted hearts and trained heads can immeasurably transform the American landscape. I lament the fact that of late, we have not heard enough regarding the impact of similar contemporary evangelistic effort, targeting the critical college cohort.

3) Testimonial

Testimonial evangelism as an evangelistic approach means that, in the main, individual saints of God share the regenerating work of the Holy Spirit as Christ is proclaimed as the ultimate hope of salvation with unsaved persons. Person-to-person outreach, in the name of Christ, represents a sure way of conveying the love and grace of God toward depraved, sinful, corrupt, wayward humanity. A personal testimony by a repentant, forgiven, enlivened sinner proves nearly irrefutable. When a redeemed saint of God offers a moving, compelling, strong declaration of what God has done, reversing a downward spiral, it allows the unsaved to see God working to rescue a life overwhelmed by doubt, fear, emptiness, and despair.

Such a convincing, successful testimony must be shared in enthusiasm, the positive act by one made alive in Christ: *"I punished them often in all the synagogues, I tried to force them to blaspheme...at midday, O king, I saw on the way a light from heaven, brighter than the sun, shining all around me...I said, 'Who art Thou, Lord?' And the Lord said, 'I am Jesus whom you are persecuting...for this purpose I have appeared to you, to appoint you a minister and a witness not only to the things you have seen, but also to the things in which I will appear to you'"* (Acts 26:11-16).

That testimony, coming from arguably the foremost proponent of Christianity in the New Testament, and, perhaps, in Christian history, the apostle Paul, provides the necessary elements for a moving manifestation by the Holy Spirit of God: 1) a sin-filled life prior to Christ; 2) the inescapable moment of surrender to Christ; and, 3) the new trajectory of life, after Christ reigned as Savior and Lord. In sum, Paul affirmed that something wonderful occurred in his life, upending everything that previously occupied his pursuits. After meeting Christ as Savior, life would never be the same again for him. The same is still true today: Christ offers radical spiritual transformation for all who embrace Him by faith.

The importance of personal testimony in seeking to win another to the way of Christ comes from the sense that, no matter what past failure, sin, anguish, guilt, or shame, if God cleanses, forgives, claims, and redirects us, then, He stands ready to achieve the same for another. In a word, the change in life prospects must be evident to the unsaved.

Let saints of God share testimonies of salvation, taking them from lives of moral bankruptcy to ones filled with passion and purpose. Let such testimonies celebrate the heavenly Father who welcomes, the Holy Spirit who convicts, and the Son of God who cleanses by His atoning blood.

4) Relational

Christian saints embracing the ethos of *"ambassadors for Christ"* (2 Corinthians 5:20) must examine their significant relationships: family, friends, neighbors, co-workers, high school classmates. These relationships offer a safe harbor for sharing the monumental truth of one's existence: life has been dramatically transformed by Christ. Due to years of conversations (covering a range of topics), people feel comfortable inviting their friends to Christian worship as one means of evangelism. Further, such friends (or family) have been able to observe another's comportment and character. As such character aligns with that of the Savior, though not in perfection, another may be persuaded of the viability of the Christian way.

To test my theory of relationships as the basis of Christian evangelism, I asked a Bible study group of 50 persons to relate the means by which God brought them to salvation and then membership in our particular Christian fellowship. All told of a friend or a family member who was used by the Spirit of God to share the plan of salvation from Scripture: repent, believe, and confess Christ (Romans 10:9-10). After recounting that spiritual change effected by the Holy Spirit, using a human instrument, I asked the responders a question: *"Did anyone come to Christ through a stroke of lightening, a meteor shower, an earthquake, or some other-worldly phenomenon?"* No one expressed what might be a "miracle moment." Rather, it was a human-to-human, everyday connection. A daring individual, heeding the voice of the Holy Spirit, went beyond the norm, reaching out to another, with the message of God's grace through Christ. Indeed, in every case, it was that simple!

Relationships, then, form the fulcrum on which life-altering change is built. To be human involves submergence in a matrix of relationships, offering safety, coherence, and guidance. Take away relationships, and we are adrift from the shore of hope, buffeted by a rough sea. Thankfully, God has connected us with so many others with whom we form lasting relationships. In that spirit, Christians should compile a listing of all those relationships. Having done so, we should inquire (if we don't already know) as to their greater relationship to God through Christ. That's Christian evangelism in a nutshell.

As a teaching tool on another occasion, I asked our Bible study group and the much larger worshipping family to provide me (in writing) with the names of everyone's unsaved or un-churched husband, wife, brother, sister, niece, nephew, cousin, aunt, uncle, grand-child. I was really stunned by the response.

That list ran to several hundred names. I announced my intention to pray for each person listed there: 1) that each would be amenable to the Christian Gospel message; 2) that our members would invite their relatives to one of our two Sunday morning worships; and 3) that a great harvest of souls would ensue from our evangelistic efforts. By the grace of God, that "family" evangelism method has produced significant results, for one reason: every saint of God in any Christian congregation in America has hundreds of meaningful relationships outside the church family. Here, again, my late pastor offered wise counsel: *"There is no shortage of sinners in need of salvation through Christ."*

Among Southern Baptists of the early 1980s, the late W. Oscar Thompson Jr. played an important role as seminary professor and Christian leader. Before his untimely death, he wrote a very helpful book, titled, "Concentric Circles of Concern." In it, he declared the driving passion of his life: sharing Jesus with humanity as Savior and Lord. In the book, he outlined the simple yet tremendous observation that the Master Plan of evangelism encompassed one person connecting every human relationship to the centrality of Christ. In substance, members of the body of Christ seek "to know Him and make Him known." While most tend to weigh down life with needless complexity, life pivots on small ideas embraced by millions.

Two quotes from Thompson make the salient point on relationship evangelism: *"The most important word in the English language, apart from proper nouns, is relationships... there are two basic relationships in life. One, of course, is the vertical relationship with the Father. The other is the horizontal relationship that we have with other people."* Forty years after it was published, that book stands as a testament to the Word of God, insight, and practicality in reaching all of our significant relationships with the wondrous news of God's grace toward sinful humanity.

Moreover, people appreciate authentic relationships based on sensitivity, integrity, trust, and recognition of their uniqueness. The Word of God beautifully summarizes effective evangelistic zeal: "Praying...that God may open for us a door for the word, so that we may speak forth the mystery of Christ...Conduct yourselves with wisdom toward outsiders, making the most of the opportunity. Let your speech always be with grace, seasoned, as it were, with salt, so that you may know how you should respond to each person" (Colossians 4:3-6). In Christian evangelism, as well as most endeavors, it holds true: People don't care how much we know unless they know how much we care! We demonstrate care for others by informing them of ultimate truth and ultimate hope in Jesus Christ, both for now and for eternity.

5) Media

Present-day Christianity pulsates with the breadth of opportunities to utilize the varied media to broadcast the Christian message of ultimate hope in Christ. Technology has almost limitlessly broadened ways to share the Gospel message. In a world of texts, e-mails, tweets, Facebook, Instagram and more, we should utilize all available media to spread salvation truths. One suggestion might be that Christians e-mail every person with the biblical plan of salvation. Then, persons could follow-up the e-mail with a personal phone call. Oops, contemporary "millenials" don't talk by phone!

When I receive an e-mail from a Christian friend, encouraging me and asking that I send it on to others, brightening their day, I always think to myself: "I'm already saved by Christ;

this e-mail would produce better results if forwarded to the unsaved." Moreover, today's media world is overloaded with information on all celebrated persons (including Christian ones). The overwhelming concern in my heart is that we harness this "information overload," directing it toward an evangelistic target: reach the lost with the wonderful claims of Christ.

As a church family, we utilize all available media to convey the Christian Gospel to the widest possible audience: radio, television, Web site with "live stream," worships, books, CDs, DVDs, printed Bible studies, and more. Indeed, I concede that I am not altogether aware of all the ways current technology allows us to connect with the larger world. Yet, a while back, I had sense enough to appoint a young member as our "IT" (Information Technology) Ministry Leader. My charge to him was simple: "Keep our church on the cutting-edge of technology, while never neglecting Christ." With praise to God, when we ask worship visitors how they came to share in worship with us, invariably they describe our inviting web presence, or having heard us on radio. In short, well-developed media drives new converts to Christ.

6) Saturation

This evangelistic approach designs a prayerful, concentrated, focused, data-driven, time-set work for recruiting the lost, and assumes that such will prove beneficial. I wholeheartedly agree with the premise. Modern political campaigns (perhaps minus the "prayerful" part) are built on that notion. For three months, say, every mailbox in a community receives a flyer with the candidates' name and photo, along with a theme or color associated with it. Often, political operatives will almost guarantee that, provided no ugly scandal emerges, the candidate who "saturates" the mail or the airwaves with his or her message will prove victorious.

In like manner, Christian leaders and their congregations could "saturate" their neighborhoods with an evangelistic "campaign." Such a campaign, regularly, beyond Easter, would aim to introduce neighbors to that fellowship, its beliefs, its history, and its warm embrace, with Christ as its apex and central appeal. Every appeal to the unsaved should be bathed in Christian love and warmth.

Admittedly, this attempt to attract new persons to the kingdom of God and new members to a particular Christian fellowship strikes some as too "worldly." Such thinkers reason that, if and when God wants new people saved, made alive and spiritually transformed, He will achieve it without human involvement. That philosophy would negate the entire premise of personal evangelism. In fact, God delights to use us as instruments of His grace toward all humanity.

Perhaps the fear that immobilizes so many Christian leaders and congregants from saturation evangelism involves concerns for secular "marketing" and the sense of "manipulation" that might occur. While I understand the reticence of many in what may seem to mimic "worldly" methods, the Christian community must always seek to maintain relevance in the marketplace of ideas and notions. Indeed, if the heartbeat behind Christian evangelism is not Christ-centered, Spirit-led and kingdom-oriented, with peoples' salvation as its objective, untoward, ungodly, un-holy things can follow!

7) Mass

Closely akin to the saturation approach enumerated above, this method emphasizes taking the redemptive message centered in Christ to a mass audience through various means (city-wide crusade, major media, etc.) For so many decades, the Rev. Billy Graham was, arguably, the foremost proponent of mass evangelism. These efforts, often in large stadiums around America and the world, generated millions of respondents, drawn to a simple yet profound message: God's grace in Jesus Christ extends to all humanity. Who can forget the compelling images of thousands of persons coming forward at the time of invitation, after dynamic worship, full of music, message and manifestation by God? Even the greatest cynic must agree that, when diverse masses respond to the sublime proclamation of Christ's saving power, and their opportunity to receive it, signals deep desire for spiritual fulfillment.

In the direct spiritual lineage of Graham for the present generation, we should applaud the mass evangelistic efforts of Pastor Greg Laurie, evangelist Luis Palau, and others, seeking to take the Christian message to the unsaved masses, both in America and around the world.

The objective of mass meetings should be the glory of God, Christian unity, hundreds or thousands of conversions, initiating the process of discipleship, all while encouraging the newly saved to share Christ with their concentric circles of contact (family, friends, neighbors, and coworkers).

In the current Christian environment, there are examples of mass Christian worships and conferences in various American stadiums and arenas (sponsored by mega-church leaders and Christian denominations). Indeed, these inter-racial gatherings happen with frequency, at exorbitant costs to participants (travel, lodging, meals, and registration). In several cases, thirty or forty thousand or more attend. Arrayed in their finest apparel, they hear great music, spirited singing, stirring preaching, insightful teaching, annual reports, while being bombarded by secular merchandizing. Indeed, much Christian "fellowship" occurs within these annual meetings. Sadly, however, few conversions to Christ take place.

The agenda does not even point to the necessity of the Great Commission. In rare cases, such meetings seem to celebrate "saved status," rather than reaching out to the lost, with the saving message of the risen Savior.

Over against mass Christian evangelism, these gatherings are mainly designed to encourage latent Christian faith rather than to initiate or stimulate conversions to Christ. So, advance of the kingdom of God suffers from a lack of overt emphasis on reaching the unsaved through mass evangelism. While the name of God is yet hallowed, the redeeming work of Christ still exalted, too often, we are missing the central, dominant mission of our Savior: *to seek and to save the lost* (Luke 19:10).

I, for one, rue the fact that Christians all too often ratchet up their fervor for God while among other saints, yet becoming almost mute before a dismal, decaying, dying world of sinners. Such unsaved persons sorely need the uplifting message of ultimate hope in the risen Savior. Saints' cachet with the unsaved involves our explosive message: Christ transforms lives, irrespective of past condition!

My passion for mass evangelism, meaning mass mobilization of the saints, stems from the biblical message that continues to resonate among those who hear it: You can enjoy new life, abundant life (John 10:10), only as you invite Christ to cleanse, forgive, own, and guide your life.

In a broader sense, when more in the Christian faith community express their vulnerabilities, even in mass settings, it allows more people to view followers of Christ as persons able to identify with the Average Joe or Jane. While aiming to emulate the Savior,

Jesus Christ, the Christian witness must never forget its core constituency: those locked in sin, guilt and shame, completely ignorant of their potential through Christ. Indeed, Christians exist to perpetuate salvation, to *"make disciples"* (Matthew 28:18-20), who follow Christ in love, faithfulness and obedience.

In consideration of the plight of the lost, they are increasingly plagued by a dangerous confluence of personal ills: ideology, ignorance, or indifference. In mass evangelistic approaches, Christ's message of salvation effectively meets this trilogy.

The ideological pitfall of pride—not viewing oneself as lost—must be addressed, as unsaved persons in this new generation live with little regard for the ways of God. Also, incredible ignorance of the Scriptures must be overcome by those who refuse to accept God's judgment upon their worldview. Further, we should be aware of the dangers of indifference—the "whatever" factor so prevalent in American culture, preventing so many from repenting before and coming to a gracious God, who offers life, meaning, and purpose through His Son, Jesus Christ.

Therefore, it seems illogical to think the unsaved world will "come to" Christian faith without hearing the Christ message. So, those of us following after Christ must "go to" the lost. Mass evangelism provides one means to genuinely connect with lost persons (family, friends, neighbors, co-workers, person X) in our midst.

CHAPTER 10

Don't Miss Evangelistic Action!

Due to a myriad of reasons and rationales, many will live out their Christian existence without presenting, let alone having someone respond to, the Gospel message of Jesus Christ. This fact is quite unfortunate, in that spiritual reproduction (leading another to salvation through Christ) is akin to the natural variety. Indeed, new converts to Christ are called in the Bible "babes in Christ" (1 Corinthians 3:1). What a high privilege we have, then, to serve as an instrument used by the "obstetrician" of grace, Jesus Christ, while God's Holy Spirit regenerates.

Despite this prominent role in leading the unsaved to new life in Christ, many saints neglect evangelistic involvement for a number of reasons. Let us briefly consider a few of them.

1) Ignorance

For some, the hesitation to engage in Christian evangelism stems from ignorance: no Christian leader (pastor, professor, denominational executive, or evangelist) ever made it clear as to

Christ's mandate and mission for the Christian church. Indeed, many have never heard the challenge to tell one person about the saving power of the Lamb of God. Or, so they say! If I sound skeptical here, it is because if one reads the Bible with any degree of consistency, our Lord makes sharing His gracious, redeeming and sacrificial work on Calvary the centerpiece of obedient Christian living. After all, the imperative to witness to the unsaved in the name of Christ is a "command," not merely a suggestion. Thus, we are under obligation to share His truth!

In many cases, it is quite convenient to lay diminished evangelical fervor at the feet of a neglectful spiritual leader. While I affirm the leader's role in pushing and prodding individual saints in the monumental task of soul-winning, I also must place responsibility on those in the pews, to search the Scriptures for guidance in evangelism. In that biblical search, I am confident that saints will discover their role in leading others to salvation.

2) Self-consumption

Other saints, for the lack of a better term, are too self-directed and self-consumed to consider the spiritual plight of another. Forgive me ahead of time, if I walk the periphery of blasphemy to argue that some saints have "too much church," while not having enough "compassion for the lost." Many Christians seem to reason: *"If I could come to salvation, surely someone, somewhere, somehow will tell the lost about Jesus."* Indeed, that represents a decidedly selfish notion. It is akin to one running from a burning building, into the safe arms of fire-fighters. Once out, these first-responders ask if anyone remains in the building. The safe person then replies: "I was so intent on getting out, I didn't really notice. But, you probably should go in and check. If anyone remains in there, I hope it all works out for them."

This self-centered sentiment, in my view, shapes the conversation of so many Christians, as they emphasize all God has done for them: healing, deliverance, blessing, marriage, promotion, victory, etc. While Christianity affords multiple benefits to the saved, God expects the recipients to share what is readily available to the lost, once they embrace Christ as Savior. Unfortunately, too many spiritual leaders "pander" to the self-centered impulse of Christians, preaching messages geared to what saints can *obtain from God* (stuff), rather than what they should *achieve for God* (kingdom expansion by new souls.) That difference in perspective explains why some congregations bask in the supernatural, while others languish in human-centered tradition. Truly, new converts to Christ energize any congregation.

3) "Lord, send a revival."

In that same vein, some well-meaning saints anticipate a "move of God," one that will prompt national revival and spiritual renewal. Perhaps a major crusade for souls will be launched; perhaps some latter-day Billy Graham, some reincarnated Billy Sunday, some new-day Jonathan Edwards will be used of God to set America on fire! So, many fervently pray for revival, to usher in mass conversions. Often, saints fail to see their responsibility in at least getting the lost to Sunday worship, or to that dreamed-of evangelistic crusade. My reasoning should be clear: if the redeemed do their part (invite, testify, and affirm), while the unsaved do their part (repent, believe, confess, accept), then, God will do His part (convict, forgive, convert, own).

Again, the desire for this mighty manifestation by the Master is commendable; but it is prompted both by prayer and by direct action by saints of God. Prayer to God without personal actions (yearning, seeking, and inviting the lost to Christ) is tantamount to desiring a meal, yet failing to cook, with non-existent groceries. It is a good thing, but nearly impossible to achieve. I often wonder: Why has prayer for some replaced tangible actions? Perhaps it is far easier to piously bow, mouthing platitudes, even as we evidence little or nothing once we raise our heads. I encourage prayer and practice: asking God to save as we intentionally reach out to the unsaved, in the name of Christ.

4) Christian evangelism seems outmoded, dated, "out-of-style."

Still others in the body of Christ, I believe, truly want lost people to come to the kingdom of God; but evangelism seems dated, difficult, time-consuming, pushy, and, maybe, a bit too dogmatic. They incorrectly reason: in God's own timing and way, He will save those who should be saved. So, they pray to God for souls, yet fail to act in the name of Jesus. Prayer without participation could be termed "benign neglect," in that desire for mass conversions is there, without overt personal engagement. Through good intentions, the lost languish in their painful alienation from God. Guilt and shame confine the unsaved to emotional enslavement. So, few hit the streets!

It is amusing to hear current saints talk of former days, when they were ardent soul-winners for Christ. I inquire as to what changed, from then to now. I often hear how challenging and hectic life today is for Christians (As if that were not the case 30 years ago). Many are now ensconced in professional achievements, too busy to tell others of their hope in Christ. So, again, few hit the streets. The cause of Christian evangelism is not threatened by assault from without, but rather from fatigue from within. Never before in the Church Age have so many saints been so "tired," or, too old, without examples of meaningful attainment. Perhaps it is just easier for some to claim they are "tired" than to engage in kingdom work. Many, then, seek vacations while negating the notion of tangible works of righteousness.

At the same time, a mere few decades ago, there were resolute Christian leaders who pushed saints, amid myriad challenges, hectic schedules, and family concerns, to centralize Christian evangelism as their highest priority. These leaders, sensitive to saints' time and lifestyles, nevertheless knew that the kingdom of God should take precedence over other mundane concerns. Their "Jesus" passion, then, overflowed in their preaching, teaching, evangelizing, and modeling of Christian behavior.

In the Kansas City area forty years ago, there was a beloved pastor who was incessant about reaching the lost: He proudly displayed large bumper stickers on his automobile, affirming the name of Jesus. (Yes, he painted the name of "Jesus" on his car!) Daily, he also wore a giant button with the name of Jesus quite prominent on his suit jacket. When anyone spoke to him, he would quickly and profusely mention Christ as the Savior. Indeed, he seemed to have a "one-track" mind as far as the priority of personal soul-winning was concerned. Oh, how I pray for more leaders like him, even in our sophisticated, enlightened, progressive, twenty-first-century Christian world!

5) The Master's mission should haunt every Christian.

Further, I submit that the church of Jesus Christ must heed the Savior's words: "We must work the works of Him who sent Me, as long as it is day; night is coming when no man can work" (John 9:4). Though ostensibly a carpenter by training, Jesus chose for His twelve disciples a decidedly "motley crew": rough, profane fishermen, a wily tax-collector, an aggressive political zealot, and a would-be thief and betrayer, among sundry occupations. Yet, the "works" to which Christ alluded were kingdom-oriented: delivering persons from spiritual darkness, through connection with Him. Among many objectives, I challenge spiritual leaders to remind the people of God of their obligation to "work" for the kingdom, instead of resting in their saved status, while millions drown in despair, adrift from security in the arms of the Savior. Greater still, too many believers enjoy saints' privileges over disciples' responsibilities.

6) The "total" picture of Christianity

In our day, we need more "work" from the saved, reaching out to the lost, rather than total absorption in maintaining sanctified status, amid the downward pull of temptation, vice, and sin. Please hear me well: Saints must live consecrated, moral, godly lives; yet, they must also discover new, creative ways to share the message of Christ with a decaying culture, starting with unsaved friends, family, neighbors, and co-workers. Too often, the emphasis has rested on simply "living a godly, Christian life," hoping that unsaved others will ask us about the source of our peace, poise, and joy. While that might occur, we should not leave the matter to chance. Instead, we "work" for Christ by intentionally sharing the details of His sacrifice for our sins. Though often garbled, confused, and misinterpreted—even, sadly, by Christian preachers—the Christian hope is clearly articulated in Scripture: "...*God was in Christ reconciling the world to Himself, not counting their trespasses against them...*" (2 Corinthians 5:19) Christian "work" today involves personally transmitting that profound truth to the unsaved, one person at a time.

7) Christ represents the only hope for humanity!

Meanwhile, many see the Christian church, particularly its African-American component, as the best hope for America, reviving the nation. Increasingly, black Christians, however, are being challenged to address issues impacting neglected communities: racism, poverty, education, healthcare disparities, drug abuse, blighted neighborhoods, "food deserts" in the urban core, domestic violence, police brutality, and high incarceration rates, amid a litany of social ills. Unspoken, in my view, is the foundational problem of American society: too many people (of every ethnicity, race, gender, class, orientation, and condition) are spiritually lost, failing to embrace Jesus Christ in daily considerations.

I heartily endorse the "social justice" paradigm for the Christian church (please refer to my book, "A Time to Speak," Walker Five Publishers, 2013). My concern in this present book, however, states the Christian church's mission and purpose, categorically: serving as the chief instrument for advancing the kingdom of God through Jesus Christ with the masses of the unsaved. Through personal transmission of the Gospel message of Jesus Christ to the lost, the black church continually expresses its relevance.

While many champion *empowerment*, the church should never neglect *evangelism*. While many work for world peace, the church must never neglect *inner peace*. While many advocate for *justice*, the church must never neglect *justification*. While many press for *civil rights*, the church must never neglect *spiritual rights*. Ultimately, Christians stand for establishment of a personal relationship for the unsaved with the unique Son of God.

My great fear for the body of Christ is that we will become socially prominent, culturally relevant, politically astute, and economically viable, while forgetting our preeminent spiritual calling: seeking the unsaved, and then enlisting them for Christian discipleship. Through the Savior, lives are radically altered, for time and for eternity. While Christians must remain conversant with all that makes for "holistic" living, we have a spiritual priority.

This world, no matter its allure or appeal, I must remind us, is not our home! The old saints used to remind us, "We are just pilgrims passing through." Indeed, I celebrate the Word: *"For our citizenship is in heaven, from which also we eagerly wait for a Savior, the Lord Jesus Christ"* (Philippians 3:20). Or, *"But God, being rich in mercy, because of His great love with which He loved us, even when we were dead in our transgressions, made us alive together with Christ (by grace you have been saved), and raised us up with Him, and seated us with Him in the heavenly places, in Christ Jesus, in order that in the ages to come He might show the surpassing riches of His grace in kindness toward us in Christ Jesus"* (Ephesians 2:4-7).

8) Evangelize the unsaved, outside "the huddle."

Several years ago, a friend reminded me that, too often, Christians resemble a football team. On the field, players enjoy comfort and warmth in the "huddle," surrounded by like-minded teammates. The comfort of this gathering is quite understandable, though unfortunate. While the next play is announced by the quarterback in the huddle, no team "scores" by remaining in its huddle. Instead, they must execute the play within the framework of the overall "game-plan," with each player performing his specific responsibility. When done properly, it represents a thing of beauty, often leading to a touchdown, field goal, or other score. On the other hand, if the team remains in the huddle for too long, it results in a "delay of game" penalty from the referee.

In my view, for too long, the church of the Lord Jesus Christ has enjoyed the comfort, warmth, and safety of its "huddle": Sunday worship in some beautiful, ultra-modern, utilitarian sanctuary. Often in there, saints are disconnected from the challenges and struggles of a vile, vulgar, vacuous world system. For two hours (or less), we hear melodious music, interesting sermons, powerful prayers, and stunning testimonies, while surrounded by fellow-travelers on our spiritual journey. Every now and then, someone is grafted into this "huddle."

Similar to the football team, however, staying in the huddle of the sanctuary by Christians carries enormous implications. First, we cannot take new territory (souls for Christ) while in the huddle. Second, the opposing forces of spiritual darkness operate outside the huddle. Third, we cannot "score" any points for God and His kingdom cause in the huddle. And, finally, the "game" was never designed to be executed in the huddle. So, one might ask: What is the benefit of the huddle?

9) Understand "the huddle"

The spiritual "huddle" may be viewed as optimal preparation for transformed people of God. Worship in the Lord's house sets the terms for critical engagement which is both declared and expected. Scripture-reading offers a formidable "game plan." Prayer to God fortifies the spirit for all that we must encounter. Songs of praise raise our morale before we must confront whatever the enemy places before us. The presence of the Lord affirms the supernatural dimensions of our undertaking. In general, the gathering of the saints reminds us of loyal allies in our fight. Thus, it should not surprise us that worship is central to taking territory for the kingdom of God.

10) Enter to worship, depart to serve.

In the old rendering, saints "Enter to worship" in the sanctuary, and then, "Depart to serve" in the streets. Unfortunately, of late, we have confused the purpose of Sunday gathering, calling that time "service." A few years ago, a man asked me how many "services" our church conducted each Sunday. I said, "None." He asked if I were engaging in semantics (tomato or "to-mato"). I finally replied: "We celebrate two worships on Sunday, while our service occurs Monday through Saturday." Please help me make that distinction!

Amid consideration of the flood of regular concerns (employment, education, graduation, marriages, healthcare, holidays, layoffs, bills, vacations, and news stories) incumbent upon all, saints of God must find time amid busy schedules to have the conversation of a lifetime with family members, friends, co-workers, neighbors, or anonymous persons. That conversation, of necessity, should point to the central concern of the ages: *"Have you accepted Jesus Christ as your personal Savior?"* Or, *"If you were to die tonight, are you certain where you would spend eternity?"* On their face, these seem simple inquiries; in practice, we know, they become intertwined with both overt and hidden implications.

As with so many probing questions, these should haunt individuals long after answers are given. If one answers in the affirmative, it should occasion rejoicing as one saint celebrates coming into contact with another. On the other hand, if the answers are negative, they should initiate a meaningful conversation, though not an argument, based on Scripture, featuring Christ as the balm for another's spiritual healing.

Throughout this book, in my attempt to encourage evangelistic engagement, I have vacillated as to the nature of my task: between appeal and advocacy, pleading and pushing, why-everyone-should and why-everyone-hasn't. To be honest, even at this point, with thousands of words, concepts, biblical, spiritual, theological, and practical principles, I am still unsure as to the best means to deploy millions of evangelical saints to the task before us.

11) Again, we need "urgency" in Christian evangelism.

What I am absolutely certain of, however, involves the notion of urgency. Every day without telling others of our faith in the Lord Jesus Christ represents a lost opportunity. We will never know how close some unsaved person may be to eternity without Christ. Daily, the news conveys untold suffering, loss of life, devastation, murder, mayhem, senseless violence, and more. Daily, millions pass on, leaving unanswered questions in their wake: Where is that nice old lady down the street? What happened to that young couple and those two children? What became of that troubled young man? *Where is that vivacious young lady? Did my co-worker come through her challenge? Did my friend ever find relief? Should I have said something to her? Could I have helped in some way?*

Most of us—saints of God, redeemed by Christ, those seeking to represent Christ—recognize the urgency of the moment. As so many die in car accidents, commit suicide, delve deeper into nihilistic lifestyles, and, generally, run out of time before calling on Christ as Savior, it behooves us to take this Christ message to all with whom we come in contact.

Urgency causes doctors to admit seriously-ill patients at once! *Urgency* means the outstanding bill must be paid, today! Urgency motivates the district attorney to arrest the active felon, immediately! *Urgency* makes car-insurance operational, the moment it is paid for! *Urgency* demands the report, right now! *Urgency* means the soul without Christ stands in jeopardy, this very moment!

Clearly, there is little benefit in rehearsing all the missed opportunities we had to share the grace of God in Christ. Yet, Christians can vow to use the next moment given to state the case for new life through the Savior. As daunting as it may be, the redeemed church of God represents the "cavalry" coming to the rescue of those unable to extricate themselves from the strictures of sin, manifested in foolish choices, wrong alliances, haunting guilt and covering shame. Because of what Christ did on "Calvary," grace, forgiveness, and hope have now arrived!

12) The Christian "call to action"

When the national security of America is imperiled, citizens expect that the president will take immediate action. To do otherwise represents dereliction of duty. His action signals to friend and foe alike our resolve as a nation. After the events of 9/11, it was only a matter of what plan, and when it would begin, that would send troops, tanks, equipment, aircraft, and materiel thousands of miles to realize American objectives in Afghanistan, the sanctuary of those who harmed America, killing nearly 3,000 citizens.

This analogy should remind the Christian faith community of its role in intentional projection of spiritual might. Indeed, God has a formidable "army," composed of those who have been spiritually transformed by the blood of the Lamb slain on the Cross of Calvary. Perhaps, today, we need a refresher course on the battle preparations of the saved: *"Therefore, take up the full armor of God, that you may be able to resist in the evil day, and having done everything, to stand firm. Stand firm therefore, having girded your loins with truth, and having put on the breastplate of righteousness, and having shod your feet with the preparation of the gospel of peace; in addition to all, taking up the shield of faith with which you will be able to extinguish all the flaming missiles of the evil one. And take the helmet of salvation, and the sword of the Spirit, which is the Word of God. With all* _prayer and petition_ pray at all times in the Spirit, and with this in view, be on the alert with all perseverance and petition for all the saints" (Ephesians 6:13-18).

13) Strengthened for the battle

When I feel vulnerable, uncertain, depleted, helpless, and devoid of strength, this passage serves to re-energize, re-ignite, re-animate and re-focus me. Further, I am convinced it will do the same for the body of Christ, as well as remind all of the spiritual battles we will face when we dare to declare Christ's saving power. The Kingdom of God through Christ advances into the hearts and minds of the unsaved, once they learn and embrace God's grace, mercy, and love.

Further, the symbolism of Ephesians 6 should remind saints of the "battle attire" at their disposal. Note that Christians are more than adequately prepared for what they will face, as they take the joyful message of ultimate hope in Christ to the spiritually lost. By God's grace, Christians possess truth, righteousness, the gospel of peace, the shield of faith, their helmets, and their swords. Moreover, these "weapons" are bathed in the power of prevailing prayer: _"For though we walk in the flesh, we do not war according to the flesh, for the weapons of our warfare are not of the flesh, but divinely powerful for the destruction of fortresses. We are destroying speculations and every lofty thing raised up against the knowledge of God, and we are taking every thought captive to the obedience of Christ, and we are ready to punish all disobedience, whenever your obedience is complete"_ (2 Corinthians 10:3-6).

When we consider the immensity of our "battle attire," we should never be intimidated by the hordes of the unsaved. As far as I can tell, most saints neither win nor lose the battle against the enemy for the "prize" of Christ converting a soul; instead, most simply forfeit the entire engagement. This situation then proves troubling. Saints experience neither the thrill of victory, nor the agony of death. Instead, they are left to wonder: What could have occurred, if I had taken the fight to the grand theater of engagement: the mind of the unsaved?

As the literal military engagements (Korea, Vietnam, Iraq, or Afghanistan) suggest, a formidable American military, while dominant, will not prove victorious in every scenario. Weather, terrain, guerrilla tactics, novel techniques, roadside bombs, superior intelligence, wise troop placement, and surprise attacks also must factor into the calculus of warfare.

14) Through Christ, the unsaved reach up to God!

For our purposes, we can rely upon the principles of the Word of God, in subduing the enemy, as he aims to maintain dominance over the spiritually lost. Over and again, he convinces them of their unfitness to enjoy the privileges of salvation through Christ. He convinces them that God bears harsh and deadly intentions for those who have fallen from grace. He convinces them that there is no way to turn back to God. He blinds them to the prodigal's insightful logic: *"I will get up and go to my father, and will say to him, 'Father, I have sinned against heaven, and in your sight; I am no longer worthy to be called your son; make me as one of your hired men"* (Luke 15:18-19).

The prodigal son (representing sinful humanity) recognized that the first step in repenting from sin involves taking personal responsibility. He said, "I have sinned." That sincere acknowledgement initiates the divinely-ordained spiritual transformation. Next, he sensed unworthiness, having squandered privileges as a son, taking integrity, honor, and a good name, to the "far country" of sinful alienation from the Father. Third, he came to grip with his fall from grace. Finally, he made one simple request: Now that I have forfeited son status, place me among the servants. In his mind, his father treated servants much better than the young man's present plight.

This prodigal, then, teaches us the importance of four realities, four ways the unsaved can come to the Master: 1) Wake up; 2) Get up; 3) Hurry up; and, 4) 'Fess up. First, he senses his need to "wake up," from the slumber of sinful alienation, after languishing too long in guilt. Second, he realizes his need to "get up," literally from a filthy pen filled with swine (pigs). Third, he recognizes the necessity of his "hurry up," having been away from home too long. Fourth, he anticipates what awaits him, after his 'fess up," admitting culpability for the terrible breach in the relationship. In the aftermath, we join in the celebrative reunion of father and son (robe, ring, sandals, fatted calf, music, dancing, etc.), the perfect picture of God's joy over *"one sinner who repents, than over ninety-nine righteous persons who need no repentance"* (Luke 15:7).

This scenario should produce mobilization of Christian troops, on the field of battle. By the power of God's Spirit, Christians fight the enemy for the lives of those spiraling downward in a cesspool of unrighteousness. Indeed, we can deploy more saints, taking the message of redemption through Christ Jesus to the unsaved. Because God cleanses through the blood of the Savior, we can encourage evangelistic engagement to the spiritually lost.

15) Christians "take action" because of God's grace.

We, further, are motivated to evangelistic action because of God's great grace and love for humanity, through Christ. In biblical and theological terms, God credits to Christ humanity's sin; and He credits to believers Christ's righteousness. Indeed, Christians celebrate our salvation in Christ, in that He saved us from the *penalty* of sin (justification); saved us from the power of sin (sanctification); and will, one day, save us from the presence of sin (glorification). Saints of God, therefore, must walk in obedience to God's Spirit, so that we will avoid, daily, the *practice* of sin.

The Word captures a vital aspect of our walk in Christ: *"If we say that we have no sin, we are deceiving ourselves, and the truth is not in us. If we confess our sins, He is faithful and righteous to forgive us our sins and to cleanse us from all unrighteousness. If we say that we have not sinned, we make Him a liar, and His word is not in us. My little children, I am writing these things to you that you may not sin. And if anyone sins, we have an Advocate with the Father, Jesus Christ, the righteous"* (1 John 1:8-2:1).

That passage, and related others, demonstrates that God gains glory, using feeble, flawed, finite creatures, though redeemed by the blood of Christ, to bring the unsaved to His kingdom. So, rather than perfection in the instrument (us), God seeks willingness for His service. Practically, this means that Christians mobilize and deploy with the military we have, instead of the perfect one we seek. Indeed, we are God's forces for evangelistic engagement.

CHAPTER 11

Ten "Most-wanted" for Christ!

Famously, the FBI targets hard, heinous, vile, long-sought, dangerous criminal suspects (drug lords, rapists, mass-murderers, terrorists, swindlers, and others) still at-large somewhere in America or loose in the world. With "Wanted" posters (often displayed in post offices nationally), the FBI makes clear their highest aim: to apprehend and to arrest for the safety of the American public, those put on their "Ten Most-wanted List." Suspects on this list represent the FBI's highest priority!

With determination to speedily capture individuals on this "Ten Most-wanted" List, the FBI expends considerable time, energy and resources. They coordinate efforts with law enforcement agencies across America, as well as globally. They seek leads, sightings, known relatives and associates, and any tidbit of information, aiming to use this "investigative intelligence," to capture these wanted suspects. Their alleged crimes make them prime targets.

While at-large, we are told, these suspects pose imminent danger to others' lives and properties. Once suspects reach this list, they are usually characterized as "armed and extremely dangerous," with persons told to "exercise caution" when approaching them.

The body of Christ can learn invaluable lessons from the FBI, strategically and tactically, as we seek our targeted audience: those lost in sin and languishing in guilt, shame, and defeat. Unsaved and still available for Satan's use, they are "extremely dangerous" to themselves and others. Arrogant in flagrant sin, living in shame, wed to a foolish idea of having "time" before coming to God, we should approach them with "extreme caution." In the name of Jesus, however, seeking advancement of God's kingdom, we must resolutely "apprehend" the unsaved. God's Spirit will convict the unsaved, leading them to the Savior.

As I survey all these words dedicated to Christian evangelism (from the earlier chapters of this book), I sense the need to provide practical means for bringing clarity to the notion. Accordingly, I pray for the most effective ways to reach the lost. As a supernatural endeavor, a successful evangelistic approach must also include biblical, spiritual, theological, relational, and practical considerations.

The Scriptures affirm our case: God *"desires all men to be saved"* (1 Timothy 2:4). *"Go therefore and make disciples..."* (Matthew 28:19). *"Go into all the world and preach the gospel to all creation"* (Mark 16:15). *"You are witnesses of these things"* (Luke 24:48). *"...you shall be My witnesses both in Jerusalem, and in all Judea and Samaria, and even to the remotest part of the earth"* (Acts 1:8).

On the bases of these Scriptures, Jesus' examples, disciples' obedience, and the cumulative weight of biblical truth, I heartily encourage saints of God to furnish names, addresses, phones, e-mails of ten people (family, friends, neighbors, coworkers, etc.), who are unsaved, un-affiliated, formerly in a church, inquiring, as special recipients of divine love, grace, mercy, and forgiveness through Christ.

Through prayer to God, and by inviting them, we actively seek salvation, reclamation, restoration and commitment for the following:

1. _____   2. _____
   _____   _____
   _____   _____
   _____   _____

3. _____   4. _____
   _____   _____
   _____   _____
   _____   _____

5. _____   6. _____
   _____   _____
   _____   _____
   _____   _____

7. _____   8. _____
   _____   _____
   _____   _____
   _____   _____

9._____ 10._____

_____ _____

_____ _____

_____ _____

Once composed, the spiritual leadership of a Christian congregation (pastor, elders, deacons, ministry leaders) should guard this list with the utmost of care. It represents members' connections, vital linkages, and a growing network of important, vibrant, inquiring persons.

At critical intervals, the congregation should specifically pray for the salvation of those so named. Also, it is imperative that a designated group ("Evangelism Ministry" workers) be responsible for keeping a current knowledge of these "spiritual prospects" for God's kingdom.

The FBI's "Ten Most-wanted" List changes due to the capture of certain ones, the incarceration of others, and the execution of still others. Similarly, the list of "wanted" souls will change, as some come to faith in Christ, others join other Christian fellowships, etc.

Most importantly, every congregation has a built-in "target-group," simply by conducting a people survey of all members' significant relationships. As with any worthwhile endeavor, such a list requires dedication, diligence, and determination before it yields tangible results. Over time, however, properly "worked," it will.

CHAPTER 12

Mobilizing and Deploying Saints for Evangelism

After writing these chapters, the logical flow expects that the body of Christ will be motivated to follow the Master's marvelous mission: *"Go, therefore and make disciples..."* (Matthew 28:19). Nothing must ever supplant this clarion call to share redemptive truth centered in the Son of God, Jesus Christ. No other emphasis in Christianity—worship, prayer, Bible study, obedience, sanctified living, giving to the kingdom, prosperity, deliverance, taking authority over the enemy, being successful, or more—stands above inviting the unsaved and the un-churched to the knowledge of salvation, by grace alone, by faith alone, in Christ alone. Until more humanity comes to new life in Christ, we practice incomplete discipleship.

In the foregoing chapters, I have attempted to convey the urgency of sharing the Christ message with the unsaved, so as to foster more conversions. At certain places, I have argued that all viable entities (schools, businesses, and families) should be able to validate their existence on the basis of tangible results. For the body of Christ, results should be both quantitative and qualitative. In a real sense, new faces in a congregation (quantitative), as well as stronger, obedient, disciplined, focused saints (qualitative) should always represent our objective as the Christian witness. As a Christian pastor, I want to honor God by yielding my life to Him, seeing more and better saints, under my spiritual care.

I do not apologize for wanting to lead more people to salvation, as I implore God's own to serve Him as "salt" and "light." (Matthew 5:13, 14) With results on my mind as a Christian leader, at the beginning of the year, I challenge our church family to help lead a specific number of souls to salvation, with those so converted coming to dwell in our church family. In corporate-speak, I share "metrics" by which we can gauge our effectiveness.

My passion for Christian evangelism stems from a bed-rock conviction: despite millions in America, and billions globally, there are still more billions in need of salvation through Jesus Christ. The lost, unsaved, and un-churched live and work among us. They are our family members, friends, and associates. They emerge from every strata of society. Yet, they need Christ as Savior! I pray some will hear that old hymn, with its haunting refrain: *"Tho' millions have come, there's still room for one. Yes, there's room at the cross for you."*

That sentiment keeps me focused on "catching" new fish, while I watch God's Holy Spirit "clean" those already in the net. Be careful of any leader, any congregation, any teaching totally consumed in "cleaning" fish, as tempting as that may be. In my view, the Pharisees, scribes, and zealots missed the point of Jesus' coming. Instead, they were consumed by "cleaning" people of God. In the process of that bigotry, the religious cognoscenti failed to extend the franchise of saving faith to those in need.

In a very significant call-to-arms for evangelism, some time ago, Wayne McDill wrote, *"Making Friends for Christ."* Early in that book, McDill illustrated misplaced priorities in soul-winning. He told of a man who led one soul to Christ. Everyone in his local church fellowship commended him on his accomplishment for God's kingdom.

Shortly afterward, he was invited before a group of churches to share the details of his successful mission. Again, they applauded his dedication to God. So this soul winner was successful, until he quit his job to solely concentrate on sharing his experience. Indeed, he wrote a book regarding the principles and pragmatic nuances of leading a sinner to repentance and acceptance of Christ as Savior. One challenge, however, became apparent: in self-reporting on his impressive deeds, he never again led another to the Master!

With that backdrop, I want to offer some keys to mobilizing and deploying saints to the "fields," (job sites, schools, restaurants, post offices, banks, service stations, online with friends, and everywhere), in anticipation of God's guaranteed "harvest" of new souls (Matthew 9:37). Please note each exhortation as the feeble attempt of a yearning Christian leader to other leaders, in hopes that the kingdom of God will be enlarged!

How, then, do we mobilize and deploy God's people for evangelism?

1) **Teach the relevant, explicit Scriptures forming the evangelistic mandate.**

After serving our church family for a number of years, I was led by God to share extended teaching on evangelism (one saint conversing with the unsaved, aiming to lead the unsaved to salvation in Christ). I asked the Bible study group if they had any inkling of what I meant. To my joy, the overwhelming majority informed me that, in years gone by, we were well-known in our city as an "evangelistic" church, with a record of extensive ways of reaching the lost (radio, television, revivals, conferences, feeding the hungry, a community bookstore, a Christian elementary school, and more). I asked what I thought was the next logical question: *"Why, then, are we not more engaged in similar evangelism today?"*

A dear sister responded to my question. Her response was classic: "Pastor, you have taught many great truths, but you haven't emphasized evangelism." I was taken aback; for, if you had asked me, I would have protested that, in my mind, all of my past teaching and preaching had been evangelistically-centered. Of course, transmission (my intended teaching) differed from reception (what people in the pews heard from me).

After gathering myself, I stated to the congregation, "I sincerely apologize if I have failed to give evangelism its highest priority. Thus, I now plan to teach only one subject, evangelism, for as long as it takes to get that concept into us!" That declaration and subsequent teaching began three years ago! Up to this point, I have shared, at least, eleven parts of evangelistic teaching.

2) **Emphasize the one-to-one nature of spreading the Christ message.**

Aim and achievement are inextricably linked. Indeed, if one seeks an end, there must be appropriate means attached. So, if the goal is evangelizing, with Christ as the message, we must utilize a "means" of getting that message to the masses. In my view, the best way to spread a good message (outside a multi-million dollar media campaign) is through one-to-one sharing of it.

As a long-time Baptist pastor with a passion for seeing more come to salvation, may I be so bold as to castigate my own denominational tradition? For too long, we have invited in a good preacher, asked him to share the Word, and called it a "revival," even as none have come to saving faith in Christ. Then, faced with few, if any, converts, many of us concluded: "Well, God just wanted the saved to be encouraged in their walk with Him." Yet, if we aim for souls for the kingdom of God, we should, by all means, season our efforts with some one-to-one spreading of the Christ message.

In the main, the practical plans for a revival meeting include developing printed materials, maybe some radio spots, and hoping some will attend. While I am sensitive to those Christian leaders and congregations who bathe the impending revival in prayer, if we fail to fervently encourage members to invite their lost and unsaved friends, the majority of efforts represent little more than regular dates on the church calendar. Often, from one year to the next, some leaders and congregations simply fill in the name of a guest speaker.

Christians should all be honest: when was the last time we participated in a prayed-up, well-developed, organized, Christ-exalting "crusade" for souls, with everyone aiming for, at least, one encounter with an unsaved person?

In our traditional mode of operation, the evangelist himself (yes, I have been invited to several churches across America to lead a revival), often never tells anyone at the hotel in which he is residing of the purpose of his visit. In my thinking, the hotel manager, a maid, bail-man, concierge, or some other person might be reached with saving truth regarding Christ.

Or, it might be beneficial if someone alerted the clerk at the restaurant of the "revival" in the city. It might lead to results if ten people in that church fellowship tried to invite ten friends and/or family members to be their guests in worship. (Each night as the guest evangelist, I ask members to invite a visitor. Then, the next night, I ask if anyone actually did so.) That way, the "evangelist" will have prospects to reach with an anointed message centered in Christ.

Not only do "revivals" or "conferences" need the augmentation of one-to-one soul-winning. Regular worship on the Lord's Day also would be enhanced to the degree that individual saints reach out to the unsaved, prior to the next week's worship experience. Then, a God-honoring, anointed, biblically sensitive, Christ-oriented, enthusiastic pastor would realize "prospects" in the pews for potential life transformation.

3) There are benefits to "role-playing" in evangelistic training.

In evangelistic training, we must avoid a simplistic rote method of sharing what Christ has done for humanity, in effecting salvation through His sacrifice for personal sinfulness. After all, Christianity immeasurably differs from a commodity to be sold, using the right technique, or the right words, as with moving computers, televisions, or automobiles. Rather, Christians, moved by evangelistic zeal, must have compassion for the target of the Christ message: lost humanity. Lost people are complex creatures, living amid guilt and shame, coping with incredible challenges. Accordingly, we must not emphasize getting the "sale," as much as bringing another out of the darkness of sin, and ushering him/her into the marvelous light of Christ (see Colossians 1:13).

While being careful to avoid "salesmanship" tactics, we must familiarize saints of God with relevant Scriptures, which serve as the central pillars of salvation: 1) all of humanity is sinful (Romans 3:23), and separated from God; 2) Sinful alienation proves costly and deadly (Romans 6:23); 3) The only remedy for sin involves the substitutionary sacrifice of Christ on Calvary (Romans 5:8); 4) Confessing and believing on the risen Christ brings humanity to salvation (Romans 10:9,10); 5) None in Christ will be condemned (Romans 8:1); and, 6) God's Holy Spirit in the believer verifies and validates personal salvation (Romans 8: 16).

Of course, the entire Bible, (particularly the New Testament starting with the Gospels), tells of God's love for sinful humanity. Yet, we can encapsulate the plan of salvation, essential to know for all Christians, and essential to convey to the unsaved, in the six pillars expressed in the preceding paragraph. These easy-to-recall verses from Paul's Epistle to the Romans, often referred to as the "Romans Road" to salvation, will greatly benefit all who commit them to memory.

Indeed, Christianity should not become routine and reduced to a formula; yet, it must not represent whatever nice, kind, and well-meaning people advocate in the natural realm. The sovereign God sets the terms for coming to Him, and that way, of necessity, must pass through His only Son, Jesus Christ (John 14:6).

By "role-playing" in evangelism training, I mean: before the class, one Christian talks with another person (in the role of the unsaved), sharing the above Scriptures. Often, in a natural way, the unsaved "actor" will try to confuse the Christian through numerous objections, delays, evasions, excuses, and questions. Then, the evangelism class should evaluate whether the sincere sharer stayed true to the Scripture presentation of the Christ message. This is the best example of "constructive," rather than "destructive" criticism. Of course, it must be handled very carefully, to avoid hurting unsure persons.

Further, "role-playing" allows Christians to sharpen their skills, expressing their hope in Christ, before a supportive audience.

4) Share specific prayer times for saints to deploy to evangelistic fields.

Nothing will change lethargy in the pews among Christian saints as much as coming before the heavenly Father, asking Him to give more of the Christian faithful a love for the unsaved. It needs to be the kind of compassion that propels more of us toward the confused, the troubled, and the burdened by the cares of this world, while being woefully unprepared for the next one.

Another problem that prayer to God will change involves disrupting a smug pew, with leaders confirming personal, insular concerns (worship, remaining "saved," cleaning flaws, prosperity, starting businesses, marriage, American nationalism), without sufficient concerns for millions who are presently unsaved.

Consider mid-week Christian gatherings, if their total focus were on intentional mobilization and critical deployment by dozens of Christians, seeking one other unsaved person with whom they may connect. Would it make the difference we seek? We will only know as we try it. The petition before God is quite interesting: saints shouldn't pray for sinners/unsaved to come in, but, that saints will go out! If this occurs, Christ assures us, in effect, that the "harvest" (new converts) will be available.

Of course, it will require spiritual maturity to attend such gatherings, knowing we will be praying for our own determination and courage. The model set by Christ in Luke 10 affirms that treacherous times await those taking the Christ message to the unsaved and un-churched. Lambs are being sent out in the midst of wolves. However, the profound Christ message transcends any challenge: "...Say to them, "The kingdom of God has come near to you" (Luke 10:9).

5) **Make banners, signage, and vision-statements of Christian evangelism prominent.**

If we pay attention, political campaigns expend millions of dollars for a few hectic weeks, getting names and faces of otherwise unknown persons before us, so as to influence our votes. Often, we will not be fully aware of the "platform" of the various candidates, even the one we ultimately vote for. Instead, campaigns rely upon steady bombardment of a name, logo, and color scheme, so as to fix in the mind of voters an association with which they become acquainted.

To be sure, Christian congregations must not imitate political campaigns, nor follow secular trends. We can, however, adopt critical cues from intense advertising: 1) Whatever becomes emphasized generates considerable interest from millions; 2) People really pay attention to a barrage of information; and, 3) If evangelism is a Christian's, or a congregational, main emphasis, it should be prominently displayed to draw all toward it.

Banners and large signage, prominently displayed in the sanctuary or on conspicuous bulletin boards, communicate at all times, even as no words are uttered. The Christian fellowship which is sincere in reaching the unsaved will waste no effort to convey this overriding concern. While talking to myself as a Christian leader, as well as others, I say: "Christians must not be afraid of experimentation in reaching out to the unsaved."

6) Remember, and re-emphasize, the "main thing" (Jesus!)

I reiterate a central premise: The overriding mission of the Christian church forever remains sharing the central tenets of our faith in the Lord Jesus Christ. Along with living a holy, wholesome life, enhancing our marriages, and seeking material prosperity, saints of God must express their highest hope in the transformative power of Christ. This lifestyle of expression, in Christian terminology, is called "evangelism." For believers, the fullness of the Christian life transcends inspiration, personal betterment, or psychological liberation; in fact, it expects the unsaved to embrace eternal hope. The redeemed of the Lord will "say so," telling others of God's grace in Christ, reversing the course of sin.

From the day of his conversion experience, at the intersection of despair and existential angst, the apostle Paul, God's "trophy of faith," continually presented a three-fold testimony: 1) His deplorable life before Christ; 2) How he came to saving faith in Christ; and 3) All that had transpired since he came to Christ. Without shame, this man incessantly shared all that God had done in bringing new life and new objectives. Brought before religious courts, civil authorities or former acquaintances, the response from the apostle Paul remained the same: Christ rescued him from a life of empty religion, ushering him into a redemptive, rewarding relationship.

Against this backdrop, I propose we analyze the phenomenon of taking a glorious message of grace, mercy, and love to the world. In short, Jesus saves! In short, He forgives! In short, the past is cleansed! In short, life becomes immeasurably enhanced by a new life of faith in Christ!

In the rush of life's demands and priorities, a friend presented a persuasive slogan for his congregation: *"The main thing is to keep the main thing the main thing."* They enthusiastically repeat it as their creed. That pithy encapsulation sums up the driving theme of this chapter. In everything, Christ represents the ultimate "main thing." All that the Christian witness entails should give Christ optimal place, in worship, music, preaching, teaching, and living.

Periodically, I challenge our congregation: We must call the name of the Lord Jesus in all that we do, every Lord's Day. I pray that no visitor leaves any worship experience without hearing us call and celebrate that name. Indeed, Christ rides above every other name. One day, every knee will bow before Him, while every tongue will confess that Jesus Christ is Lord.

7) Christ represents total sufficiency.

In that proclamation of Christ, we affirm Him as totally sufficient for every culture, class, and condition; totally sufficient for every person, problem and perplexity; totally sufficient for every heart, hurt, and humiliation. Yes, He is the main thing for all.

Theological controversies may draw the Christian church's attention and agenda, but neither involves the "main thing." Often, Christian denominations (Catholics, Baptists, Lutherans, Pentecostals, Charismatics, Word of Faith, or Independents) hold to many differing biblical interpretations, dividing the body of Christ, bringing hurt to the heart of our Lord; but we must not neglect the "main thing."

With the words of 1 Corinthians 9:19-23 burning in our ears, I exhort more Christians to joyously following the Master's mandate: win the lost. In the vernacular, we should vow to win some, reorienting persons to the way of faith in God, fostered by the Lord Jesus Christ.

Let's win some broken people. Let's win some bruised people. Let's win some beaten people. Let's win some sad, suffering, sullen people. Let's win some who are "good" or successful by the world's standards. These are often the most difficult to reach because, in their reasoning, they are not sinners! (Too often, they confuse bad behavior with sinfulness). As referenced in an earlier chapter, the unsaved, or sinners, are those devoid a relationship with God through Christ.)

By every means, we must win some!

8) Pragmatic dimensions of sharing Christ with the unsaved

If we accept Christian responsibility to "win some," the question becomes, "How?" What are the strategic considerations and tactical dimensions of the work? What should we do, specifically, in reaching out to unsaved, un-churched, unsure hordes all about us? How do we share God's unfathomable love, grace, and mercy? Those inquiries demand answers. I propose to offer such answers in this chapter.

In the world of advertising, we hear about the "optics" of a particular presentation. The concern is not what others should know; but, what, in fact, others see from our presentation. Too often, in the Christian witness, the optics point to a worldview of smug, satisfied, stuffy, sedated saints. We sing of joy, even as our facial expressions belie such. We affirm that our confidence rests in Him, while the smallest personal challenge occasions howls of despair.

Returning to the specific tactics of evangelism, we open our mouths, among friends, family, neighbors, and others. Tactics, of course, connect with and flow from strategic considerations. The strategy is to present the love of God, mediated through the Lord Jesus Christ, to all humanity, irrespective of background, behaviors, or baggage.

9) Christians "win some," by these principles:

☐ Become a slave to the human condition; we are interdependent.

☐ Live from the perspective of the lost—fears, failings, and frustrations.

☐ Listen with an ear of sensitivity—barriers to belief.

☐ Help others understand Christians as a caring community.

☐ Know that the kingdom of God yet expands, for His glory!

10) Celebrate publicly tangible results of evangelistic engagement.

In the local church setting, it is critically important that Christian leaders celebrate those who are new to the Christian faith, as well as those new persons in the church fellowship. I am clear as a Christian leader: except for a few ministries (elders, deacons, trustees, or stewards, or the "board of directors"), new members should be warmly embraced as potential candidates for service to God, depending on spiritual maturity level, dedication to God, willingness to serve, commitment of time, energy, and material resources, and more. In this way, we aim to "make disciples" for Christ, rather than simply getting decisions.

We base our "philosophy of ministry" on cultivation, establishment, maintenance, and enjoyment of relationships with people, unsaved and saved.

Here's a reality check: church people are risk-averse when it comes to engaging with unsaved people. Part of the risk involves Christians being reminded of what God delivered them from (violence, alcohol, drugs, nightclubs, sexual promiscuity, profanity, negativity, and more). So, those still ensnared in such sinful, ungodly behavior are to be avoided at all costs! Thus, evangelical fervor is sapped, as we shun the very people our Savior spent His time elevating. Note Christ's circle: *"Now all the tax collectors and the sinners were coming near Him to listen to Him. Both the Pharisees and the scribes began to grumble, saying, 'This man receives sinners and eats with them'"* (Luke 15:1-2).

As Christ's followers, seeking to advance God's Kingdom in human hearts, can we rightly disregard persons with sordid pasts?

Let me share our intentional evangelistic strategy: on a Sunday morning, as God's Spirit directs, with extreme discretion, I call forth a new convert to Christ, one new to the congregation. While hugging that person around the shoulders, I will announce his or her name before the audience. Many wonder as to my aim. It is simple: I am publicly calling attention to his or her conversion experience, resulting from some one-on-one encounter, where this person responded to the Gospel message of Christ delivered by a committed saint in the congregation.

If Christian leaders and congregations seek to mobilize and deploy saints in evangelistic engagement without celebrating the results, some might wonder as to the effectiveness of our efforts. Similar to a car dealership reminding salespersons of cars sold in a given month, only with our kingdom achievements having eternal implications, we must connect soul-winning with new converts, and new additions to the fellowship.

Accordingly, I am principled and pragmatic: the objective for the dealer is to sell vehicles backed by the integrity of the parent company. Increased sales motivate the sales staff, as well as generating new customers.

In the kingdom of God, the body of Christ fights lethargy and malaise by intentionally seeking and assimilating new converts into a dynamic Christian fellowship, one where God is exalted, Christ is affirmed, the Spirit obeyed, the Word enjoyed, as people are affirmed in Christian love.

11) Work hard to encourage evangelism.

In sports, I have heard coaches utter a mantra: "We just work on getting better." No matter how successful, the coach must continually keep before the team its immediate (next game), and its ultimate objective (championship). 60 Minutes recently profiled Coach Nick Saban of the University of Alabama. After winning four college football championships, he was asked his coaching philosophy. He replied: *"We aim to get the players to execute according to the principles we espouse every day."*

Saban's players recognize drive, focus and intensity in him, compelling still, even after unparalleled success.

Likewise, a Christian leader should convey through every utterance, action, and philosophy an undying compulsion to share the grace of God through Christ with every living creature, thereby bringing glory to the heavenly Father: *"I tell you that in the same way, there will be more joy in heaven over one sinner who repents than over ninety-nine who need no repentance"* (Luke 15:7).

Hard work fuels achievement in any endeavor, and especially in Christian evangelism. Hard work's companion is "smart" work. So, a church family might target a specific group for a specific season (let's reach men; let's reach single parents; let's reach young adults; let's reach the needy; let's reach young professionals, etc.)

Now, clearly I can imagine some who will rebuff me: "Collier, if only evangelistic results were as easy as you make them appear." That type of challenge amuses me, because many would rather explain why an idea will not work, rather than implement a wide range of tactics toward reaching our shared objective—making disciples for Christ.

12) Engage church leadership staff, leadership structure, and ministries in evangelism.

My late friend, Dr. E.K. Bailey of Dallas, told me that despite leading a large congregation there, he still expected and vigorously articulated to his staff of "pastors," that each must bring new converts to Christ, and to that fellowship, in order to remain employed. Obviously, it was not that harsh, or stark; but, if you knew the man, you couldn't be sure if he really meant it. Yet, the results were always there. It was a model I tried to adopt, as it was built on principle from the Word ("make disciples") and pragmatism (everyone in a Christian fellowship, deriving innumerable benefits, has equal share in responsibilities for its perpetuation).

Over the years, I have personally adapted that reasoning to the numerical growth of our fellowship: ministries' leaders should aspire towards new faces in that ministry. Just holding on to those already committed sounds feasible. However, what happens when people get sick, discouraged, tired, confused, or when God calls them to eternal rest? Thus, every ministry replenishes itself on those we deliberately "win" to Christ.

Unfortunately, I have discovered in too many Christian venues, when the intake of new converts to Christ is minimal, people there tend toward negativity, bickering, gossiping, fault finding and other manifestations of "fleshly" thinking. Many then resort to feeble attempts of "cleaning" old, rather than "catching," new ones. By design as a Christian leader, I aim to douse and dilute toxicity in the body of Christ by a deluge of new saints for the kingdom of God. Theoretically, one could drink a bit of poison if it were contained in enough water!

When "winning some" captures the Christian witness, the world will see our enthusiasm and expectancy for eternal life.

CONCLUSION

Over the last 30 years, the notion of mass Christian evangelistic engagement by faithful saints of God, reaching out to the unsaved in the name of Christ, has focused my entire attention. It also has galvanized my "philosophy of ministry." Further, it has crystallized in my ministry outreach as a pastor, preacher, author, leader and influence in the kingdom of God. Of course, I attribute its focus in my mind, heart, and will to conviction from God's Holy Spirit. I glorify the heavenly Father for every idea that rivets attention on the sacrificial, vicarious death of the Savior, Jesus Christ.

Since modern evangelism's initial awareness (in the late 1960s) and during its emotional gestation (the last four decades), I have felt a heavy burden to write down several concepts which give shape, texture, and substance to something all Christians affirm, while relatively few practice.

Christian evangelism represents saints' ultimate mission, yet easily forgotten daily task. We have, by this book, sought to change that reality.

Please note my best spiritual gifts and major assets in Christian ministry: preaching the Gospel of Christ and writing. Self-definition oscillates from *"preacher who writes"* to *"writer who preaches."* The preaching gift, given by God, has been understood and utilized now for over thirty-five years; the writing gift, from the same Source, has been nurtured by Him for over twenty years. They are compatible gifts, in that once God gives an anointed, biblical, well-researched, polished word for the edification of a congregation, conference, or some part of the body of Christ, I feel compelled to share those spiritual principles, in written form, with an ever-widening audience. Humbly, I sense the national and global implications of God's calling to take this message to all. Like a full-course meal, prepared to feed many, I seek more than a few to enjoy the "feast of the Lord."

Yet, this book was, paradoxically, among all works, the easiest and the hardest to write. In the first part, the Scriptures, concepts, allusions, and illustrations flowed; while, at the same time, I felt great resistance. The easy part was listening to God's Holy Spirit, as He must dictate revelation, illumination, and application. The hard part was encountering demonic barriers, inhibiting movement from concept to expression to implementation. So many times, I reached an impasse.

Not surprisingly, Christian evangelistic engagement, the absolute mission of our Savior as He seeks to advance the kingdom of God, should pose an existential challenge. If this work has been successful, a remnant of the Body of Christ will be moved to share the Christ message with unsaved friends, family, neighbors, co-workers and others. That one sentence embodies the central thrust of the book you hold.

Reflecting on it, I believe we have covered a great deal that potentially may serve to awaken, motivate, inspire and deploy more in kingdom service to God. More than mere, "Good job, Collier," this book yearns to engage saints in reaching the lost, connecting with the unsaved, engaging in old-fashioned "soul-winning"! While I appreciate rave reviews, I sincerely pray that saved persons connect with unsaved others, through Christ, resulting in dynamic spiritual transformations. That's the whole objective.

Christian evangelism, then, represents far more than an interesting topic; more than a good sermon series or Bible study lesson; more than a debatable notion. Instead, it epitomizes Christ-oriented truth put into everyday action. The sensation I hope this book has shared with every reader, the mission of reaching unsaved persons with the message of Christ, has been wonderfully encapsulated in a Kirk Whalum song: *"Falling in Love with Jesus"*. Note its lyrical sway:

> *"Falling in love with Jesus,*
> *Falling in love with Jesus,*
> *Falling in love with Jesus*
> *Was the best thing I've ever,*
> *Ever done.*
>
> *In His arms, I feel protected,*
> *In His arms, never disconnected, no, no*
> *In His arms, I feel protected,*
> *There's no place I'd rather be."*

In tough, trying, and taxing times, facing challenge, stress, despair, loneliness, loss and disquieting moments, it should serve as tremendous comfort to remember the early sense of *"falling in love"* with the Lord Jesus. The goal of Christian discipleship, of course, involves *"staying in love"* with the Savior, despite alluring from the enemy and one's own flesh. Telling the lost of that love rekindles the emotion, over and over, ad infinitum.

Finally, I am convinced this book begs for a sequel. Perhaps an interval must pass. Like motion pictures, I pray the sequel will be even better, and more engrossing, than its predecessor. May God be praised, and may you take the glad tidings of the Savior "to the ends of the earth."

So, please help me tell the unsaved about our gracious Savior!

BIBLIOGRAPHY

The following Bibliography captures helpful spiritual resources, by way of authors, articles, books, workbooks, lectures, and references which augmented this work. I highly recommend these resources to all for further study, reflection and edification.

Bachus, Wilma N. *The Need for Urgency of Outreach and Inreach in the Sunday Church School*. Nashville: Townsend Press, 2014.

Carson, Ben. *One Nation*. New York: Sentinel, 2014.

Carter, James E. *Help for the Evangelistic Preacher*. Nashville: Broadman Press, 1985.

Coleman, Robert E. *The Master Plan of Evangelism*. Old Tappan, NJ: Spire Book, 1963.

Cocoris, G. Michael. *Evangelism: A Biblical Approach*. Chicago: Moody Press, 1984.

Fish, Roy J. and J.E. Conant. *Every Member Evangelism for Today*. New York: Harper & Row, 1976.

Gladwell, Malcolm. *David and Goliath*. New York: Little, Brown and Company, 2013.

Gray, David L. *Does Jesus Christ Live in Your Heart?* Kansas City, KS: Witnessing Publishing, 1977.

_____. *Every Christian Is a Soul Winner*. Kansas City, KS: Jesus Christ Loves You Publishing, 1981.

Gray, David and Helen. Dr. Caesar Clark: *The Man, The Preacher, The Pastor, The Evangelist*. Kansas City, KS: Jesus Christ Loves You Publishing, 1982.

Hill, Edward V. *A Savior Worth Having*. Chicago: Moody Press, 2002.

_____. *Victory in Jesus*. Chicago: Moody Press, 2003.

McDill, Wayne. *Making Friends for Christ: A Practical Approach to Relational Evangelism*. Nashville: Broadman Press, 1979.

Moss, Otis III and Otis Moss, Jr. Preach! *The Power and Purpose Behind Our Praise*. Cleveland: The Pilgrim Press, 2012.

Murray, Cecil L. "Chip." *Twice Tested by Fire*. Los Angeles: USC/Figueroa Press, 2012.

Rodriguez, Samuel. *The Lamb's Agenda*. Nashville: Thomas Nelson, 2013.

Rusbuldt, Richard E. *Evangelism on Purpose:* A Planning Guide for Churches. Valley Forge, PA: Judson Press, 1980.

Sanders, J. Oswald. *The Divine Art of Soul-winning.* Chicago: Moody Press, 1960.

Thompson, W. Oscar, Jr., with Carolyn Thompson. *Concentric Circles of Concern.* Nashville: Broadman Press, 1981.

Vines, Jerry. *Wanted: Soul-Winners.* Nashville, Broadman Press, 1989.

York, Amos. *Soul-winning: Every Believer's Calling.* Tulsa, OK: Vincom, Inc., 1995.

CPSIA information can be obtained at www.ICGtesting.com
Printed in the USA
LVOW05s0906031214

416767LV00004B/4/P